Support for *He Transfor*

In a world that is increasingly individualistic it can be challenging to access a sense of safety and connection. This book creates a wonderfully accessible and reassuring framework that is truly inspiring, compassionate and much needed.

Dr Sula Windgassen PhD MSc,
Health Psychologist and Director of Mind Body Blossom
Clinical Health Psychology practice

A must read for individuals who want to discover and seize the silver lining in chronic pain. It is a vital tool for people working in community, health and social care, therapists and HR managers. Readers are gently guided through the author's popular Healing-Centred Design practice delivered to the public sector and business through her company 'A Brilliant Thing CIC'.

Michaela Lavender, Managing Editor
Public Money and Management, a highly-respected
international journal covering finance, policy and
management issues in public services

Kerry's book is full of the warmth, generosity and a depth of knowledge and curiosity that she exudes herself and is a real treasure trove to delve into and come back to over a lifetime of navigating the twists and turns that we face. There are both practical and magical guided elements and this books gives us the ultimate permission to take care of ourselves and the world around us however that may be ... a mighty and compassionate force for change and perfectly timed.

Lory Povah, Creative Health Consultant

Mend, Tend and Change the Future

HEALING-CENTRED TRANSFORMATION

Kerry Tottingham

First published in Great Britain by Practical Inspiration Publishing, 2025

© Kerry Tottingham, 2025

The moral rights of the author have been asserted.

ISBN 978-1-78860-773-5   (hardback)
      978-1-78860-774-2   (paperback)
      978-1-78860-775-9   (epub)
      978-1-78860-776-6   (Kindle)

All rights reserved. This book, or any portion thereof, may not be reproduced without the express written permission of the author.

Every effort has been made to trace copyright holders and to obtain their permission for the use of copyright material. The publisher apologizes for any errors or omissions and would be grateful if notified of any corrections that should be incorporated in future reprints or editions of this book.

EU GPSR representative: LOGOS EUROPE, 9 rue Nicolas Poussin, LA ROCHELLE 17000, France Contact@logoseurope.eu

Want to bulk-buy copies of this book for your team and colleagues? We can customize the content and co-brand *Healing-Centred Transformation* to suit your business's needs.

Please email info@practicalinspiration.com for more details.

Dedication

This book is encircled with love: Laurence, my sisters, family and all our children, thank you.

To The Brilliant Thing community, this book is for you.

Dedicated to my mum, the original brilliant thing.

Contents

Welcome ix

Chapter 1: Doorway one: Pain 1

Chapter 2: Doorway two: Principles 39

Chapter 3: Doorway three: Process 69

Chapter 4: Doorway four: Practice 117

Chapter 5: Doorway five: Your power 157

Appendices 197

References 199

Index 207

Welcome

An invitation to belonging

Dear person who feels deeply, who knows what too much and not enough feels like, all at the same time. I, with my heart and my mind and all the galaxy of experience that is within us and waiting for us, invite you.

I invite you to belong, here on these pages.

I invite you to a house of transformation, a place where we can change things. Come with all your gathered ideas, emotions and imaginings. Please bring your hurts and your pains, your insight into the things that need to change, your humanity. You have so much to offer, learned at your edges, living on your wits – you are brilliant already.

I know other places feel uncomfortable, that the world isn't shaped for you and the challenges you face. My chronic pain opens a window into your experience. There are similarities between limiting conditions, trauma, injustice and painful experiences, and we all carry painful parts – but know your experience is uniquely yours. We can keep each other company, meet and walk into change together.

In the house of transformation, we can design, make and create lasting change. Face our own resistance, support the kind of change that feels powerful and positive. Change in our lives, communities and society. Can you change the world? Yes! So many people have dismissed your aspiration but here it is so welcome. You are potential, you are possibility, you are change, and there are stories here to uplift, inspire and elevate your next move.

Doorways and thresholds

Doorways and thresholds have been placed in this book to represent transitions through change and move you from one place to another, appreciating both beginnings and endings. I hope you discover the resilience and wisdom that waits there for you and feel held and supported by this book to think and feel, explore and learn.

There is a rhythm as you move through the doorways and thresholds. Each doorway opens with a poem to wake up your imagination and set the tone for the following chapter. Each threshold is a place to pause and absorb learning, which includes:

- A diagram to land key concepts.
- A case study to explore how others work with pain to create power.
- A reflective practice activity to ground your learning.

You are invited to write poems, draw, make notes and collect reflections as you move through the pages, gathering a rich collection of your own insight, ideas and actions. We call these your treasures.

You'll leave with power, my friend. Your own individual, inner power activated, and with another invitation, this time to a party. This book will create momentum. Beautiful, empowering power, brilliant collective power. You choose the day, the place, the time. Savour time to read, pause to let things sink in or take purposeful action straight away – it's all welcome. This invitation doesn't have a time limit and you are in control of what happens next. When you are ready to create transformation, these pages belong to you.

Mend, tend and transform

You want things to change, but do *you* want to change things?

There is always a turning point, a moment that changes you from passive to active. A shift that empowers you to move from the 'being done to' experience to the one doing things, taking steps, raising your voice, making a difference.

Change is many things; a complex weaving together of experiences, thoughts and actions. Your change might include a blend of chronic illness, experiencing motherhood and a creative flare. Another's change recipe might blend experience of injustice, love of dancing and a knack for throwing a party. We are all a combination of complex parts and change reflects this intricacy. There is usually emotion stirring the pot too; an angry refusal to accept or a joyous lightning bolt of possibility. Change begins in shifts and the energy that shifts ignites, often making us desire radical and overnight change. Healing-centred transformation offers something different – it moves not in shifts but in transits. No less bold or impactful, this transformation-focused change looks after you as you change, move and develop. Transformation creates deep change, and mending and tending are the cares and attention needed to make this change last.

Mend. This word evokes needles and thread, darning and stitch, hammered wood, patching holes, making new, repairing. The word 'mend' has such a human quality. It's not about throwing away, replacing or ignoring problems. Mending means paying attention to the broken parts, adding something new to repair and make usable. Often the mending is visible, showing where things are worn and where they are strong again. I have an old wooden workbench in my kitchen, the joining mends telling stories of its maker and adding to its solidity and worn beauty.

If we want to change things, we have to mend what we can, as we go. Mending isn't always a physical act. Think of the emotional mending we do: the mending and adjusting of our thoughts; the mending and repairing words following a breakdown in communication. In a workplace rife with sexism strong action might be needed, but there will also be relationships to mend, ways of doing things that need to be adjusted, a cultural undoing and redoing.

Our culture glorifies people-fixing; you can buy products and services to 'fix' almost every body part. When these products break, we can snap our fingers and get a new one. Mending is not the same as fixing or replacing. It's the intentional care we apply to revitalize and make good again.

Tend. This is a directional word – it makes something happen. An untended fire goes cold, but tending a fire, over time and with the right fuel, makes it burn bright. An untended garden will be tangled with weeds. There might be a beauty in its wildness, but with tending and nurturing fruits can be grown, seedlings flourish and wildlife blooms.

When we are on the change journey, mending things along the way, we need to spend time cultivating solutions too. Tend to potential, tend to imagination. This might look like learning, experiencing, feeling and noticing. Like mending, tending is intentional effort applied to something, but instead of care being applied to problems, tending is applying this attention to solution growing.

We can't think, create or imagine in a vacuum, so tending means being with people and ideas, trying new things, tending to our own creative nature, expanding our perspectives, cultivating knowledge and connection. When I am pottering, arranging, cooking, playing, organizing, reading, imagining, looking, I am filling up my stores of possibility, nourishing potential, creating memories I can draw on and ingredients for ideas I haven't yet tasted. This is why a creative and reflective practice is such an essential part of healing-centred transformation. It's the generative, innovative, unique part where are ideas are born, and tending helps cultivate it.

Transform. When writing this book about change, I wondered if transform was too lofty a word to use. My own insecurities whispered, 'Who was I to proclaim transformation?' Yet the word 'change' wasn't quite right; change for the sake of changing isn't what this book is about. It's about change for a purpose, change that matters, change because it's personal and needed, change despite adversity, change because of it, change because you are the person who can make it happen.

'Trans' means to take something with you and 'form' means to shape and create. This book is about using the experiences that you have had in life. The challenges, pain and adversity along with your innate natural creativity, curiosity and unique perspective – using these qualities to create lasting change. Solutions created by the people who understand the problems deeply because they are closest to it. The word 'transform' describes this beautifully – you take what you have and use it to shape what you want and what the world needs.

Healing-Centred Design

Why transform?

Around a third of the world's population experience chronic pain and approximately two-thirds experience injustice. Personal pain and societal pain, exacerbated and caused by damaging systems, inequality and trauma. Imagine the momentum if all these people gathered and supported each other to change how the world works.

This central transition, chronic pain to collective power, is one I'm obsessed with. It's the transition – pain to power – that I believe underpins all change work. When something hurts us or we feel like we have no agency or option, we feel powerless, but when we feel power – personal and collective – we can create change. Victim to warrior, attacked to activist, passive to participator, critic to creator, manager to leader.

The movement of pain to power needs resilience, community and creativity, and it needs structure. I call this a frame to dance within. The framework expressed and used in this book is called Healing-Centred Design. Frameworks can feel rigid and cold, management devices, detached from the human and the context, but this one is different. Imagine a trellis with sweet peas braided around its structure, or the intricate structure of coral with its marine habitat and tendrils of seaweed. This is how Healing-Centred Design feels to me. It's a framework that connects wellbeing and justice and centres humanity. It's a reaction to burnout culture, disempowering systems and power dynamics that can be scarce and harmful. It's a stand against having to choose between health and fulfilment.

At my company, A Brilliant Thing CIC, we use Healing-Centred Design to create innovative ways to dismantle inequality and channel positive, collective power in workplaces and communities. My sisters (who work in the company too) and I use the framework to shape the work we do together and support our family dynamics. I personally use the framework to manage my health condition. It's adaptable!

The framework is focused on the central transition – pain to power. Pain gives us wisdom, insight and experiences to channel. Power, personal and collective, moves us to our desired destination, which is often about creating freedom. We have found this destination compels people and communities no matter what the context, creating freedom within your chronic health experience, releasing from the pain of toxic management, liberation from inequality, freedom to choose. We can hold the destination lightly and you can layer in your own desired outcome in words that resonate with you, but we all know the real magic, growth and impact is in the journey not the destination.

Supporting the pain to power transition and moving it from theory to action are processes and practices. Processes are steps to get us there. Practice is the way we do things along the way. At A Brilliant Thing CIC, while co-producing system change with communities we designed ways of working that support the pain to power transition.

Central to these ways of working, practices and processes are the principles created through our trauma-informed work, which are used to support transformation and change in healthy, nurturing ways. Personally, as an artist, leader and someone living with chronic pain, these principles are my go-to inspiration, resolve and painkillers:

- When I feel chaos, I reach for 'rhythm and ritual'.
- When I feel confused and overwhelmed, 'filter' shows me the next right step.
- When I feel stuck or broken, 'collide and align' releases and repairs.
- When I'm hurting, 'transition' guides me out of the dark.
- When I feel lonely, 'contribute and benefit' connects and grounds me.

Using the Healing-Centred Design framework has multiple benefits, helping clarify and communicate what matters to you and look after you and others while creating change. Perhaps the most useful outcome of using the framework is that it keeps you going, keeps you believing in a world where justice is possible and pain doesn't dominate, because apathy is one of the biggest blockers of change. Possibility, energy, connection and inspiration are accelerators of change and natural outcomes created through the practices and processes of Healing-Centred Design.

I've woven my own and other people's stories into these pages too, which feels vulnerable and empowering. You'll see and feel my experiences as a way into exploring your own. I hope that by being honest and open about my feelings and thoughts, allowing a glimpse into my personal world and those people who inspire me, you'll see how profoundly these practices and processes can impact on your interior world as well as your external environment, work, community and society you live in.

With the Healing-Centred Design framework and principles, you can:

- Practise working with pain, so you can create more possibilities.
- Develop processes that increase your energy.
- Embody and share power and connection.
- Discover ways to activate power and create ripples of inspiration.

Threshold: Healing-Centred Design framework

The Healing-Centred Design framework and principles guide transformation from pain to power, so we can make a lasting difference to things that matter to us, mend the things that hurt us, tend to and nourish our inner strength and rise to the challenge of change-making together.

Healing-Centred Design framework

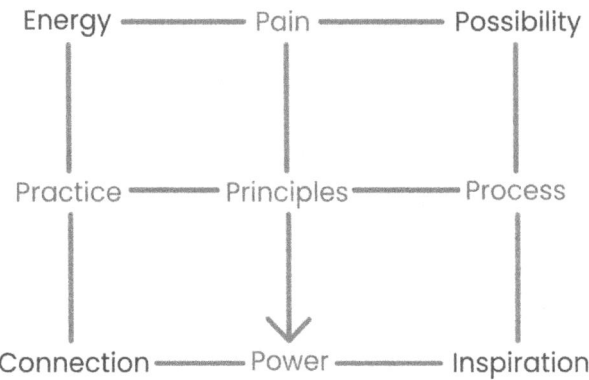

Case study: Dr Sula Windgassen

Dr Sula Windgassen is a clinical health psychologist and researcher specializing in chronic illness and mind–body health. Her work emphasizes holistic, patient-centred care, blending compassion with cutting-edge psychological and health research. Dr Windgassen lives with chronic illness, using her personal experiences to inform her compassionate approach.

'Wow!'

I flopped onto the bed where my sister Faye and her eight-year-old were lounging after an early morning swimming session, telling her all about the chat I'd just had. They were upstairs giving mum some space to spend time with her friend and listening out to intercept carers at the door. I'd been up since 5am, an early start means uninterrupted time – a scarcity at the moment. I am currently working online in my childhood bedroom, 250 miles from my actual home with books, medical supplies and my nephew's travel cot piled around me just out of screenshot.

'I've just had the most brilliant conversation!'

My mum has terminal cancer and we are caring for her; my two sisters, Faye and Tess, and me. This book was written under the looming shadow of this illness and yet despite the darkness we are in right now, we laugh and enjoy seeing mum, we hot desk around the house, and sometimes we have brilliant conversations.

This was one of those times. Nearing Christmas, Dr Sula Windgassen had joined the call in a room festooned with tinsel and in front of a green-bauble-filled tree. I was excited to speak to Sula; she is a regular in my Instagram feed. I like how she gently encourages with her deep knowledge and honest approach. As a clinical health psychologist and researcher, she specializes in chronic illness and mind–body health and has lived experience of managing both. I felt at ease despite the chaos of cancer at our house, the shiny tinsel in her background sparkled on my screen and lifted my mood, creating a safe place to smile for a while.

And we began with safety. Sula explained that the word 'pain', in her experience, is shrouded in the need to feel safe, protected from threats. Pain creates and responds to dysregulation, bodily, societal, emotional pain all creating a heightened threat-detecting response. What is surrounding pain often feels hostile too. We spoke about the influence of unsupportive workplaces, societal conditioning and life circumstances that can exacerbate pain.

I think in pictures, and one was illustrating live in my mind – a gloomy pain cave and fearful work to get armoured up in the murky darkness. Ready to step out into hostility, fight, prepare to be hurt. Maybe it was Sula's compassionate presence or her clinical experience that let me imagine this horrible pain cave; usually I would dismiss and push down that type of image. But the next part of the conversation led me out of that picture and along the healing path that this book travels too.

'What if it's not armour or fight that is needed?'

I explained to Faye that Sula told me about three states: the rejection of pain, enmeshment with pain, and a third state, me plus pain. In rejection, we hate pain, hate being a person in pain; we are in a fight stance or distance ourselves as far away from pain as possible. In enmeshment, pain becomes our whole identity; we think of only pain – we are pain. In this perspective-shifting third way (me plus pain), we are ourselves alongside pain. Interesting.

Interesting and so much alignment with how people respond to societal pain. Rejection can look like ignoring or denying issues like poverty or racism, or blaming others without seeing our own role in changing the things that cause pain. Rejection can also look like the pious 'helper'; helping the poor person but never recognizing our shared humanity. Enmeshment can feel like giving up, apathy, overwhelmingness and passively encourage us to become part of damaging systems despite having an awareness of the pain they cause – who am I to change anything? What about this third way then? Me plus?

I wondered aloud, 'What keeps you there, living in the regulated zone of me plus my pain?' Paying attention to your thought stream was Sula's reply, and I imagined a river of thoughts flowing out of that pain cave. I had the urge to jump in, float downstream with the pacey current, be whisked away, lost in ideas. But I caught her words at the last minute, 'Choose when to listen to your thoughts', and was tugged back to the conversation. Pay attention to your thoughts and your body when you are physically or emotionally stretched. When you are in pain, your thought stream might not be the place to immerse. In the regulated 'me plus pain' zone, I am aware of my thoughts, but also my body, my needs, my vast internal landscape, and I can choose. And choice paves the path out of that cave.

Before I wandered down that path, Sula threw me a ball. A basketball in fact, well, the story of one. Back in her NHS days Sula regularly played a game in her office of Self-Compassion Basketball. Players were invited to throw a screwed up ball of paper through a hoop on the wall and would win a point if they scored while sharing a self-compliment. A running scoreboard tracked the compliments and points and a practice of self-compassion and fun built in the office. I threw Sula a ball too, in the shape of a 'Boast Book'; a weekly team practice of sharing and writing down a boast to normalize celebrating ourselves and others. The Boast Book was born when I was working in the NHS too and a colleague from that time recently shared that she still uses the practice. It's powerful to remember that small and memorable moments, with groups of people, can shape lasting experiences at even the most complex institutions.

The pain experience is often turning inward, and barriers to giving to anything other than our own pain can be overwhelming. Fun seems insignificant, laughter unimportant or even inappropriate. The pull to escape in waterfalls of thought and be swept away from our hurting lives is strong. But the conversation with Dr Sula was not about pain. It was about power – pain and power living alongside each other. Choices to gently turn outwards, welcome receiving support, scope out possibilities, listen to our bodies, share our feelings, move with compassion, retreat sometimes to regroup and then emerge with the feeling of aliveness.

Dr Sula Windgassen reminded me, in the dark of our family pain, in my raw physical pain and in the shadow of societal crisis that swirls, we need knowledge and action, but we have another need too, for compassion. In this complex mix, the glow of light, tinsel and a disarming smile can exist here too.

www.healthpsychologist.co.uk/

Reflective practice: Invite in

What is it?

Invitation is our first step into transformation – invitation to step through an open door. To create a meaningful invitation we need to pause, observe and give space for possibilities to take root. I think of this type of reflection as being like pulling back the bow, holding the tension and preparing for release.

How do I do it?

Take some time to reflect on what brought you to this point in your life. You might need to find some quiet space to think alone or share your thoughts with someone you trust. Use these thoughts to write yourself a simple, heartfelt invitation to visit the 'house of transformation'. You don't need to know exactly what that means yet, just that you feel compelled to work on healing and transformation. Free write your hopes, dreams and wonderings. Let your words flow without judgement and add doodles or sketches in the margins. When you're done, read your invitation aloud, and let the act of speaking your words be the moment you invite yourself into this process of change.

What next?

This invitation is the beginning of your reflective journey from pain to power. Through activities in this book, you will be encouraged to build a collection of reflective artifacts. These might be written notes, drawings or objects. You can draw on these when times are tough or when you want to validate your progress. Choose a pouch, folder or special drawer to gather your artifacts in and keep them safe.

Next, we are going to explore pain and find wonder at its edges.

1

Doorway one: Pain

You're at the entrance of the house of transformation, walk through the stone arch softly lit against the night sky. Read this poem slowly and look up.

🗝 Grit: A poem for resilience

When you say my grit is not enough
Or the pearl is too shiny,
Ignoring the tender bed,
The craggedy fluted shell splits,
Blade shucked open, pool of water within.

A pearl moon reflected.
A dark ocean of night,
Inward, twilight settles.

You know moon, with steady gaze.
You see, you stay,
In dark water gleaming.

When you say my grit is not enough
The shell is too shallow,
Carved grooves worn on the inside.
The pearl should not gleam,

The water should not swell,
The night should stay black.

I look up at pearl moon poised,
And I know.

By Kerry Tottingham

It's not that bad

Stepping through the night and into this book, I only found these words because I walked a path forged by pain. Chronic pain and societal pain, both symptoms of injustice. Healing through pain, transforming pain into the grit, support and collective power we need to change our lives and the world. This is a change journey all can walk.

I'll begin with a memory, filed away in a cupboard called 'It's not that bad'. Lying on the floor with jagged glass splinters in my bladder, I told myself it's not that bad and reached up to type out a vital email that had to be sent by 6am. Then I had an out-of-body experience. Maybe it was the hardcore painkillers or the lack of sleep, but I struggled free of my body and looked down. I watched myself crumble, trying to hide from the pain and still get my to-do list done. Desperately digging in my mind for ideas to make things better and knowing this was not the story I wanted for myself.

I wanted a meaningful life, one where I was nourished, supported and free from pain. A life where I am calm, connected to others and creative. A life where creativity is coming from somewhere light rather than being gleaned from others or driven by the need to escape. Endometriosis and chronic bladder pain are not the building blocks you would choose when creating a meaningful life.

From medical gaslighting to emergency boiling hot baths, to dealing with doctors who told me with a pat on the head, 'They want to help because I'm a nice lady', I could easily sink into a limited life. In fact that was the prognosis and advice from doctors, colleagues and friends. Pacing, limiting, doing less, living smaller. But with a history of overcoming personal trauma and many years working in the non-profit sector, I had enough evidence that transformation was born out of adversity. A flicker of inspiration kept my imagination alive — what might my life be despite this pain, or maybe even because of it? As well as the medication and treatments that I hoped would mend my body, I knew I needed to tend to that flicker too and build a fire.

To picture where I spent most of my time, imagine a Venn diagram of self, support and society. While managing chronic pain, I was knee deep in self-development, leaping at just enough opportunities to support health and body to stop me crashing and had set up a social enterprise with bold ambitions to change society and how we work.

Why wasn't I resting? I was asked this often enough for doubt to seep in, and I tried. I tried relaxing, eating well, sleeping. But the pain always chased me from my bed, pounded in my ears as I watched the weather through the window or attempted any other rest activities that were recommended to me. Healing through rest felt as solitary as the pain, and nothing ever changed in isolation. I was running from lonely pain, taking every 'doing' opportunity to escape.

Needing to not be alone, and with community in mind, the nagging question, 'What might my life be?' changed to 'What might our lives be?' then to 'What could we all be?' I knew there were lots of people out there who experience pain. Every time I tentatively shared online there were 'me toos' in my direct messages (DMs). In fact, between one-third and one-half of the UK population (just under 28 million adults) are affected by chronic pain according to the National Institute for Health and Care Excellence (NICE).

Health research studies show that meaning in life predicts the functioning of those patients in pain. In my work life, in community organizing roles, I have seen how contributing through activism, volunteering and community building not only benefits society but also has valuable, lasting benefits for the people involved. Doing good stuff makes us feel good, feeling good helps with pain, sharing good stuff creates more of it for everyone. I wrote this sentence in my journal and opened up my imagination.

For many of us, the world tells us to limit ourselves, either through conditioning, discrimination or through the oppressive messages we absorb. It's no wonder that our bodies absorb trauma and respond through physical pain. But what if healing from this conditioning, creating changes in society, putting power back in the hands of people who have felt the effects of pain, injustice and inequity could be the most powerful painkiller possible? If this hypothesis was true I was going to have to get comfortable with pain and stop running from it.

Anatomy of pain

We are walking alongside each other now, and you may be wondering who I am. I am a mother, sister, daughter and wife. I am maker, a writer, daydreamer and thinker, a company builder, facilitator and social change designer. I am a person healing from trauma and living with pain. My flavour of pain is chronic; it's in my pelvis, my bladder, my internal experience. It's imprinted with sexism, generational pain and experiences beyond my control. I have endometriosis and another condition that sounds so nebulous it feels made up, but it causes screams of crushing pain – bladder pain syndrome.

Your flavour of pain might be physical, emotional, environmental, structural, social or organizational. It's the thing that keeps you up at night, which hurts you and that you have fire in your belly to change.

I am a straight White woman. I am married with a blended family. I can support myself and others financially. I have many choices. My generational trauma is not genocide, or structural racism, or systemic oppression. I experience the privilege that our culture provides for people that meet certain criteria. I own my pain story and I do this work as an ally to others' pain stories. I will not take on others' stories and insert myself or centre my understanding in their experiences. I hope the work of this book is to develop personal power in each reader, contributing to collective power together.

One of the most hurtful things about pain is that it isolates. There is an old idea that floats around when I talk to people about sharing pain stories. An idea that pain, openly shared, will infect others. Society is quick to blame, shame, call selfish, dismiss or admonish as attention seeking. Other people will often be incredulous when you share your pain. 'There must be a fix?' 'They need to find out what's wrong!' Over time, after many invasive, intense procedures that don't work, you tumble through broken layers of medical systems, clutching your diagnosis letters to prove your experience and hiding the impact while smiling through well-meaning advice. So we build walls, hide our pain, shrink from it.

If we are going to channel pain into the power that will create change for ourselves, others and our world, these walls need windows. To know pain, in its many forms, we need to see each other, create windows into others' worlds and doors to spaces where we can gather. This window into my world is an opportunity to open windows into yours.

I am committed to trauma-informed working, but I don't call it that. Placing the word 'trauma' into spaces where we need more healing makes it hard to create the gentle lightness needed. I hold the boundaries of healing-centred work to design spaces for people to create without the pressure of injustice, spaces to learn and develop skills to manage external pressures themselves and spaces to decompress and process the impact of working in an unjust society.

Dr Shawn Ginwright, Professor of Practice at Harvard Graduate School of Education and the author of 'The future of healing: Shifting from trauma-informed care to healing-centered engagement', states:

'A healing-centered approach is holistic involving culture, spirituality, civic action and collective healing. A healing-centered approach views trauma not simply as an individual isolated experience, but rather highlights the ways in which trauma and healing are experienced collectively.'

The pain that we can turn into power is multilayered. It's the inner pain that our bodies create a container for. Chronic conditions, emotional and physical health challenges, acute pain caused by injury or disease, addiction, inflammation and its tracked connections with past trauma. It's also in the outer pain, the pain we see in our families, friendship groups and communities. The damage of financial insecurity, social weaknesses and infectious illness. The damage we do to ourselves, self-sabotaging behaviours reacting to external triggers. The pain people inflict on each other through crime, hate, abuse and othering. It's the public pain. The pain of living with oppressive systems, decision makers motivated by greed and unjust power, sprawling global companies that have designed humanity out, damaging societal norms, unhealed historical trauma – repeated.

Inner, outer and societal pain. Each causes harm to the individual, the group and the society. We cannot separate these pains. For example, the public pain of discrimination, chained to the outer pain of socio-economic inequality, tangled with the inner pain of depression.

Spending time with pain, knowing it, understanding its roots and interdependencies, rather than avoiding or running from it, is the first step to healing. To understand pain we need to expand outside of our own experience and explore how we got here. So, who are you? What is your complex and multidimensional experience of pain? What shaped and influenced it? What can the particular texture and blended colours of your experience reveal? Can you see any chinks of light, possibilities of release, opportunities for change, growth and development? Be gentle, but stay and explore your pain, notice and tend to it – it has much to teach you.

Conditioning

We are on our way to the house of transformation, but we need to pop into the house of conditioning first, just so we can let go of any conditioning weight we are carrying and move forward with more freedom and ease.

When you were small you probably visited the house of conditioning; you might have even lived there. In this house, they lied and told us the house was solid, secure. As long as you stayed within the walls of class, religion, the nuclear family, looked and sounded right and kept up with other norms and expectations, you would be safe – it was perfect!

They told us the rooms had names, and you could open a door when you needed something. 'Library' for learning, 'Bedroom' for sleep, 'Kitchen' for food, all available, all as it should be, as long as you played by the rules and did the right things (you know, easy things like be quiet but speak up; sleep when you want to wake up; do everything as you're told even if it feels bad; don't be greedy but do eat everything on your plate, etc). If you didn't stay within the rules or if your story didn't fit comfort, sleep and food, well, it might be harder for you to have those things – conditioning doesn't think you deserve them.

The house had many floors. We were told in school that we had to move up to the work floor if we wanted money, a job, safety. We knew the government floor looked after the house; the law was for safety. We trusted the NHS floor to take care of our health. These institutions were held in high esteem, even when we saw them hurt people; it was not our place to influence. We were certain that the charities dotted around the building (they didn't get their own floor) meant there were good people who could help the whole house if needed. If we were lucky or deserved it, we found our way to rooms for art, music, sport, friendship, entertainment and hospitality to enrich, comfort and nourish us.

There were people in the house, talking about how much better things used to be, telling stories of better times, better people. We felt like we were somehow doing it wrong; doubt festered in this house. Conditioning is run on fear, the undercurrent of loss, scarcity and hurtling into despair, each damaging experience perpetuating a yearning for a golden past.

When you have freedom, you don't have to live in that house anymore. As an adult, you can open your eyes to conditioning and see the gilded past never really existed. With conditioning as the driving force, we are taught that racism, classism, inequality and opportunities are available to the privileged few and that injustice is inevitable. With freedom, we see equity is possible.

Evidence of conditioning is everywhere. Here are some examples connected to health:

- The NHS can't help with debilitating, unresearched conditions and often disregard mind–body connections.
- Embedded sexism through lack of opportunity for women's progression in medicine and within treatment options means conditions like mine are dead ends.
- Underfunding blighted women's health, underrepresented groups' wellbeing and medical issues affecting those who could not advocate for themselves (or access the power that would listen to them).
- Traditional health charities were based on the power imbalance of the helpers and the helped, reinforcing structural classism, racism and inequality.

Where does conditioning lead? To hungry children, fragile wellbeing, using and users, people falling through gaps into dark holes, filling emotional gaps with scrolling, next day delivery consumerism.

These are not the kind of doors I want to open. I want us to feel free. In a world where trauma, pain, inequality and injustice are everyday occurrences, making dreams a reality can seem like a privilege that only a few can access. But that's the sneaky voice of conditioning. Our conditioning quickly turns the blame inward. If only we could be more, work harder, do more. Or we fight and blanket-blame, shaming ourselves or the world until the dream becomes a cry, then a silent wail with a bitter gaze. The reality is that the system is often stacked against us – *but we can use this as fuel for change.*

Stay with the conditioning house metaphor and imagine moving homes, creating three piles: keep, let go and recycle. Intentionally choose what to take forward in our transformation journey. Travelling lighter and moving forward, we can unpack and rearrange, try out different layouts, find the best place for rest, family rituals and muddy boots. We can place filters at our new doors, removing poverty, racism, inequality of opportunity and experience. Our windows could open on to gardens of choice, abundant with fruits and flowers and spaces to play.

Moving houses

The old house of conditioning was never built with scaffolding or for access. For many people doors were locked, corridors blocked, rooms hidden and a divisive upstairs and downstairs system segregated us.

Creating a new home might mean open plan or layout maps for everyone. It might mean adaptable spaces, quiet areas and places for reflection. The garden might be important, along with places to gather and organize. Storage and supplies need to be considered and how we move around the spaces. 'Education', 'Health' and 'Crime' rooms might need to be replaced with 'Listening', 'Creativity' and 'Decision making'. A solution to an education, health or crime challenge might be found in collaborative spaces that value learning through different perspectives and in inclusive ways.

This house makeover cannot be done in 60 seconds. We don't have endless time but let's not rush and replace broken with rickety. Let's pause before we begin to build.

Pause and consider how personal scaffolding (the support we each need) gives us strength. Strength to contemplate revolution, innovation and possibility and what we might need along the way. Pause to consider the new house we could build.

Freedom and commitment

We have become intimate with pain, close to conditioning, in touching distance of freedom. The house metaphor illustrated the importance of where we live, the place from which we experience our lives and how it shapes us. We not only live in physical locations, but also in emotional worlds, in thought patterns and with others. Our internal and external world is shaped by both freedom and restrictions, layers of possibilities and obligations. Some environments are more constrained than others, hemmed in by others or our own limitations.

When I am minimized, trapped or contained, I find my fight and voice. But when those limitations are of my own making, or things I cannot control, I like to reframe restrictions as commitments. For example, my body hurts and I can't find the energy for work turns into I'm committed to pouring caring energy into my body especially when she hurts. Even if I can't change my physical environment or the limitations and restrictions around me, I can pay attention to where these restrictions are coming from and ask questions:

- Is it conditioning that tells me I have to carry on when I'm hurting?
- Can I use my imagination to think of different equitable ways of living?
- Are there alternative ways of experiencing the world?

I remember the first time I realized that I had choice in how I experience restrictions and being almost immediately overwhelmed by a vast sense of freedom, like wobbling on a cliff edge with a wide ocean beneath me. Living small had reduced my capacity to feel truly free and I longed for it to change. I wanted liberty, freedom, possibility. This perspective shift and longing caused me to make wild and sometimes thoughtless choices, possibly ones I wouldn't make again. Chasing the feeling of freedom can be as unhelpful as running from pain and I've learned the importance in staying grounded through change. Are you questioning if you should be responsible for making change happen, or even wondering what right do you have to change things?

Our rights might be chosen for us. The right to work, learn, express ourselves, make choices and how we spend our time. Maybe history defines the rights we have and the benefits we receive. There might be moral and legal rights, norms and expectations that we live within. There might be judgement or ethical principles attached to these rights; an agreed position on what is right and wrong. Our responsibilities, too, may be predefined. Accepted roles in the place come with their own set of standards and rules. Within these rules, responsibilities might allow us choice, decision-making power and come with accountability; being answerable to others. Responsibility may be intertwined with care, responding with purpose to look after something or someone, to protect from harm or ensure a certain path.

It's easy to see how oppression impacts on rights and responsibilities in big ways and more subtle experiences. For example, racial profiling denies certain individuals the benefits of fair and unbiased treatment and perpetuates racism. When people face censorship, intimidation or punishment for expressing their opinions, it undermines the fundamental right to freedom of expression. A workplace where only management can access a training budget yet all are expected to continuously improve is a place where people are unlikely to feel equality. Responsibilities can become inequitable duties. In a society with discriminatory gender biases a woman might be expected to take full responsibility for caring.

I want to show you some ways that help us think about rights and responsibilities in new ways, ways that open up space for equitable power. If you work in a team or spend time in groups or communities, you might find new ways to do things here. We are all part of the big team we call humanity, so even if these ideas are not things you can directly try out, you can notice when you are a participant in bigger systems and groups, and with new ideas shape things from the inside out. I want to share these early on our journey, as they are ways of doing things that you might not have thought of before (especially if you grew up in the house of conditioning). I hope they light up your imagination and beam in hope.

Participatory organizing

Participatory organizing involves actively engaging a diverse group of people who are connected to a topic in the choices that are made and action that is taken around the topic. It's an approach that is becoming increasingly used in grant making and work between communities and statutory organizations like schools or councils. Participatory budgeting, decision making, citizens' juries and community priority setting are often elements of social change organizing.

These are some methodologies and approaches that share principles that revolve around more inclusive, adaptive and participatory ways of organizing:

- **Sociocracy**: Deciding together with agreement and circular structures.
- **Holacracy**: Teams manage themselves, no traditional bosses.
- **Deliberative Democracy**: Everyone discusses and decides on community matters together.
- **Teal**: Teams focus on what's important, caring about everyone.
- **Appreciative Inquiry**: Work highlights strengths, positive conversations and imagines a bright future.
- **Emergent Strategy**: Collaborative adaptation for significant, positive societal changes.

Unlike top-down approaches, all these methods value the input, perspectives and experiences of all individuals involved. The focus is on relationships, collaboration, listening and developing together.

Restorative justice

In a restorative justice framework, both the person who caused harm and the victim are active participants in the resolution process. The person responsible takes responsibility for their actions, acknowledges the impact on the victim and the community and works towards making changes. The victim expresses their needs and helps decide how the harm can be repaired. *Theatre of the Oppressed* is a creative approach to restorative justice that encourages people who experience a social or political issue from different perspectives to explore and challenge it through drama and performance. Developed in the 1970s by Brazilian playwright and director Augusto Boal, it turns the audience into active participants, inviting them to step into the performance and work through the struggles people face in real life.

Co-production

Co-production is a methodology often used to design and deliver new services that work better, particularly in health and social care provision. Co-production is where the creating and making of a thing (service, project, event, etc) is done with the people who will benefit from it and involves everyone who is impacted by it, including decision makers, communities and other providers. Successful co-production begins with work to explore rights and responsibilities of all involved. I prefer to use the words contribution and benefit, helping individuals consider, 'What will I contribute?' and 'How will I benefit?' Working to explore how we will collectively contribute and how we will collectively benefit. This initial thinking and choices made help maintain motivation and progression through the co-production process, highlight hidden inequalities within the group and embed equity of experience.

Alternative organizational approaches that decentralize power use inclusive practices and are driven by purpose to create commitment to change. By prioritizing participatory processes, people can shape decisions and 'home grow' outcomes. With healing-centred transformation we reject oppressive ways of organizing. We create environments that prioritize freedom, joy and diversity, role modelling for the equitable society we are creating.

Daydream

In the previous chapter we explored pain, conditioning and organizing. We expanded our thinking and have more ideas to draw on. Now let's begin to explore what matters to you. Reflection helps us find and mend the holes, challenges and snags in our lives. Daydreaming is active reflections' floatier sister, perfect for tending to our needs and our hearts and waking up imagination.

When I am in a daydream, I am most often transported to water, waves, pools, oceans and rivers. I practise slipping into daydream as a way to stay creative or move away from pain. Like now, looking out of a wide window I can see the sea. A vast ocean deep with shoals of shimmering fish, washed coral and wisps of whale song echoing in the waves. I start thinking about the whales as I daydream, their leathery blue skin and currents created by huge whale tail twists. Some people want to save the whales. This thought breaks and I follow the crest of the wave. What do I feel? I care about the whales, I do. But what I really care about is the people working to save the whales, and I remember how they helped the world fall in love with this big blue being.

Did you know whales sing to each other? I first heard this on a podcast called *Invisabilia,* which was all about the unseen forces that shape our world – perfect escapism learning! I learned about this humanizing trait along with the story of scientific understanding, awe and empathy that created an environmental movement 50 years ago. The movement was symbolised within a best-selling song, '*Songs of the Humpback Whale*', which led to the 1972 Marine Mammal Protection Act, marking the end of large-scale whaling in the United States and saving several whale populations from extinction. From song to salvation! Today, the campaign 'Save the Whales' is working towards a Global Oceans Treaty. Those are amazing transformations and a great example of the kind of outcomes transformation change can create.

Take any topic you care about taking action on, such as systemic discrimination, social justice, healthcare inequalities or your own health and wellbeing. Healing-centred transformation outcomes that include positive change are what you are striving for: policy change, public opinion change, changes in power, changes in behaviour, changes in lives, changes in how you feel. Stories like the whale song can help you have confidence in your aspirations and know that tangible outcomes of change are possible.

Floods of revolution

In the story of how people moved from not caring about whales to the public outpouring of emotion and transformation of the whale and human relationship, the bit that intrigues me most is *how* it happened. How did the song create such massive change? What created the human to animal understanding? How did it create the moments that inspired awe? What are the patterns that created empathy?

I have questions, too, about the activists behind the campaign: Scott McVay, a poet and philanthropist, Navy engineer Frank Watlington and scientific biologist Roger Payne. How did they keep going when the world didn't care and people were systemically killing the whales? What role did music play in their lives before the whale song? How did they develop ways to work together when they worked in such different professions?

When we ask questions about the people, the processes and the practices, we explore how we might create revolution too. By understanding the 'how' we widen our imaginations and perspectives. New possibilities emerge and we can design how to get to revolutionary results, over and over again. But we have to learn to ask 'how' questions each time a challenge occurs. Different people, times, challenges and contexts change the answers. The certainty is not in finding replicable answers, it's in finding replicable questions. Let's take up the position of the explorer and let intrigue and curiosity guide us; a radical act when we have been told what to do and how to feel by conditioning all our lives.

Scrap the helper

Look around, explorer glasses on, maybe with a jaunty hat and a handmade map. Can you see pockets of justice and difference emerging? Do you notice people using new platforms and conversations to illuminate change work? Do your explorer eyes see emerging ideas, a growing confidence that change is possible? It's incremental, sometimes slow, but alongside an accelerated digital world and hyperlocal community work, I can see people committed to learning; people learning out loud and open-source sharing of information.

My bookshelves heave with books on justice, DIY action and creativity. Mavericks and change makers leap out from my phone screen and shout out their stories. Through these stories I hear striking, underpaid workers fighting for justice, #Metoo movements. I see Camerados' yellow badges encouraging us all to look out for each other, cultural institutions waking up to historic and structural racism, footballers taking the knee, prime time telly thinking about representation, record numbers of social start-ups and community interest companies established and New Zealand banning conversion therapy.

I see outstretched arms wanting change, justice, equality and resilience. There is energy feeding a movement. Complex, but possible. There is war on screens too: more pain, more injustice, anger and apathy. A shiny TV campaign whips us back into feeling powerless, hoping our donated pounds add up, promising aid.

The movement for transformation and the charity model of aid are not the same thing. One is active, the other is passive and can reinforce the damaging systems of injustice that created the problem in the first place. The change you want will not happen if we all stick to traditional roles of helper and helped, benevolent and poor, healed and damaged. Instead, we need to rethink what help means. I believe it's a dance between contribution and benefit, for both sides. A charity worker who does not benefit (financially, emotionally, practically feeling valued, supported) will soon burn out and will not be able to contribute to the cause.

A social enterprise that reaps the benefits from its work but does not spend time contributing to the cause it was set up to benefit will soon be cancelled, if not by the regulator then by its customers and supporters.

Have you ever held your hands in the air for a long time? Try it now, feel the effort it takes. Imagine being alone in a room, shouting for what you care about, holding a big placard up. Now, feel that room filled with people, holding banners with their message, contributing their experiences, emotion, pain, hope to the cause in solidarity. A crowd with its arms up together has a whole different energy.

Change needs all those outstretched hands. It needs a critical mass of people and they all need to be giving *and* receiving. Mutual benefit, reciprocal contribution.

We need to build the energy of the crowd and create organizations that pulse with momentum. We need to build numbers of people and layered stories that communicate truth. We need to create places where mutuality giving and receiving is safe and trusted.

I call you to work out where you give and make sure you also receive there – demand it. Because the big, powerful change we crave, the change that will enable healing across all of our lives, begins with an intentional shift inside ourselves, recognizing that we too matter.

Pain management

That kernel of belief that you matter too can be nurtured by reflecting on your own journey and taking care of yourself and your needs. When I first started working in the social change arena, as an artist for a charity, the challenges seemed so stark and the work we needed to do was so raw. We were using inspiration, community art making, creating therapeutic spaces for making, painting and exploring. I was fresh and unjaded; the path to change was fluid. But when we started knocking on doors, talking to doctors, government services and funders, explaining how these creative and supportive spaces were so healing, how with some resources and working together more people could change their lives, no one listened.

We tried to explain that when someone felt confident to make marks on paper, choose colours and shapes, express and share their thoughts, they started to heal internally too. We explained that this was only possible if the systems and services around them, and their social networks and families, all created space and time for this development; people needed state support as they healed. We explained that sometimes the healing might take a whole lifetime, that the root causes of their pain needed to be addressed too. We gave examples; damp, mouldy housing did not align with optimistic change. We explained that smoothing cognitive dissonance, making people's outside world feel more like their inside inner world was starting to feel, would enable them to heal quicker.

I thought that by connecting these dots, pointing out the needs and getting people on board to fix problems, change would happen. At the time I couldn't see the intricate web of conditioning, historical and systemic patterns that held these damaging circumstances and unequal situations in place, dripping with thick gloopy oppression and welded with murky controlling power.

I feel this murky power run through my body as pain takes hold again. Screechy and jabbing with a heavy underbelly propelling me from bed and into a burning bath again. Read. Read and distract, fill up with idealism and learning and ideas. Imagine. Reading in the night after several tramadol in a hot bath was my escapism and the doorway into my imagination. I read books about social change and books about healing pain. I read books about starting businesses and books about revolution.

Sometimes the change work seems so clear, then other times when pain seeps in the clarity has soft edges, thinking feels heavy, movement slows and things get stuck.

When in pain, change feels like treacle: gloopy, sticky, pouring slowly and clinging to surfaces. It's so hard to create change when this pain keeps sticking and seeping and gunking up everything we try to do. Sometimes pain stops change, its viscous quality resisting movement, coating everything we do. Emulsifying, spooning painkillers, blunting sensations, dulling feelings, scrolling through lives, avoidance – these are the easy reach fixes that we might use to ease pain.

When I finally had a name for the pain that had been screaming through my body, I read every book I could get my hands on. Most of the 'cures' these books advocated for required limiting and pacing. Doctors gave me medication to stop my periods and dull my nerves: antidepressants, anti-inflammatories and finally opioids. One book that really helped listed potential alternatives to painkillers. Unlike pain management driven by medications, this list included holistic, creative, spiritual, intellectual and physical alternatives. Rather than prescribing to a problem, this was a list of potential solutions to experiment with and explore. I could make my own list and work my way through it, giving back some much needed control and a sense of progression. I'd avoid the scattergun approach and could add all the well-meaning advice to the list if it felt right, trying different alternatives in turn. I encourage you to make a list of all the possible ways to manage your pain in the moment. I want you to know this is not the end of the story but a way to find relief and cope so you can get to the other side of the pain.

My list included:

- Massage
- Rebozo wrapping
- Hypnotherapy
- Heat therapy
- Cold water swimming
- Counselling
- Self-coaching
- Acupuncture
- Sensory therapy
- Writing
- Homeopathy
- Circuits, bootcamps and exercise classes with women that make me laugh
- Astrology and mysticalness
- Various vitamins and supplements
- High fibre diet
- Intermittent fasting
- Intolerance testing
- Mood tracking
- Food tracking

- Yoga
- Being gentle and kind to my body
- Art making
- Pottering around the house
- Learning and reading and listening to inspirational podcasts

There was learning along the way: massage showed me how often I don't speak up while I'm in discomfort; hypnotherapy taught me how other people can project onto me. Tracking in various forms felt so appealing and obvious but is hard for me to do consistently, which gave me a few sticks to beat myself with. Supplements promise reassuring relief but come in ugly bottles I want to hide away!

My personal prescription for pain management now includes, heat therapy, art making, weekly counselling, monthly coaching, astrology, intermittent fasting, oat milk, exercise classes, mystical imagination, writing, learning, haircuts, time alone, pottering and aloe vera supplements.

Along with Prostap injections, HRT and slow-release tramadol, I have a range of ways to manage my pain. It's worth saying, the pain meds alone help in the moment, provide relief but do nothing to release me from the grip of the conditions. With the range of more holistic support I now treat myself with, I am healing and can manage the pain far better.

I wonder, what would a management list look like for social pain?

- Rejection – friendship
- Loneliness – community activities

- Exclusion – advocacy
- Abuse – resilience through therapy
- Discrimination – justice and accountability
- Stigma – inclusive environments
- Marginalization – boundaries and understanding
- Alienation – connection
- Betrayal – trust through social support networks
- Isolation – empathy and support from others

What if we eased social and societal pain through:

- Rest
- Making mood boards instead of rules
- Setting priorities as a community
- Cross generational mentoring
- Designing for joy rather than to fix problems
- Circular economy schools

These ideas focus on connecting, imagining and making – a trio of powerful painkillers that move us from feeling powerless to being inspired and emboldened. There are many more things I could list. You will have many ideas to add and build on, and you have the ability to discover and gather more. This gathering and collecting approach will help you as you move through these pages, take notes, highlight and underline, doodle in the margins, set up a workbook for yourself, whatever works. Change is happening and you are going to want to document it.

Whole life healing

Your growing sense of mattering holds the power for whole life healing.

Have you ever had life coaching? Often you begin with a wheel tool that contains eight areas of your life segmented for you to score. From family to spirituality, with ten being highest, how do you rate your life? Discerning where we are, so we know where we can go.

Five star review

This 'life score' activity got me thinking, 'Where else do we rate our experience?' In doctor's surgeries I've scored my pain, in supermarkets I've rated the checkout person. Uber drivers rate the passengers and passengers rate the drivers. I've given stars and numbers, typed compliments and checked boxes. Once on a ferry trip I filled in a 'How was your trip' comments box with a rambling, joyful poem about my honeymoon, hoping to make the person on the other end smile; sadly, I didn't get a reply! We score things that matter to us and to gain understanding, or because there is an incentive or benefit. But scoring alone only tells part of the story. Evaluating, asking why and delving deeper into an experience is where real understanding can be found. The number score can be a way in.

Here is an exercise to try called 'Unfold your story'.

This sensory coaching activity can be used instead of a life wheel. Crumple up some paper then smooth it out and notice the shapes made by the folds and creases. Imagine each space created is a piece of your life experience, viewed from a slightly different angle:

- Which areas would represent family, work, home?
- Big expanses or ruched areas?

- Could you fill each randomly created space, outlined by a fold, with something that matters in your life?
- Can you fill in the big sections and the small spaces?
- What does this tell you?

Radiating out from each of these core needs are supporting needs. The core need of sleep has supporting needs including a bed, warmth, comfort and safety. Food might need a place to cook, a shared meal with friends, buying or growing the food. Fill up the spaces with these supporting needs; use the back of the paper if you run out of space.

Sometimes the healing is in the supporting needs under the core needs. Picking a brightly coloured scarf when you have been conditioned to wear clothes that minimize you could represent a huge move towards healing. So get into the subtleties, use this as an opportunity to take a step back from your experience and discern how your needs are met.

Hurting bodies

Healing often happens in the subtleties, in the needs under needs. This is not recognized in the approach taken by the traditional western medicine model that often seeks to fix rather than prevent problems. In this medicine model, it most often treats the symptoms not the causes and is concerned with the structure and function of the body, particularly musculoskeletal health (bones, muscles, tissues, ligaments, joints). It involves diagnosing, treating and preventing disorders or dysfunctions. We are conditioned to believe this is the only and right way to heal.

Have you ever gone to the doctors with a virus and been refused antibiotics (because they don't work on viruses) and been angry about this? This shows the conditioning of fixing is so strong that we even override the doctors with our certainty in the diagnose-then-medicate model. Even when there is evidence that medication doesn't work, we feel cheated if we don't get a simple fix. Back pain is a stark example of the 'fix' approach not working. Back pain investigations often find a problem in the vertebrae, doctors medicate with painkillers and operate to fix. Yet in the USA, back surgeries are successful only 60–80% of the time. There is a huge opiate crisis caused in part by overprescription of painkillers and in a stringent research study published in 2006, only 22% of patients were satisfied with the outcomes of surgery two years later. Diagnose– medicate–operate is not always the answer to hurting bodies.

Pain prescriptions

In society, we try to fix pain in this way too. Take a huge systemic and multilayered problem like social inequality. A traditional model to fixing a social problem might follow a similar diagnose–medicate–operate path. To fix a social problem it seems logical to assess, intervene and restructure. But this can have the opposite effect, as illustrated by a recent catastrophe in the UK.

The Grenfell Tower fire in London resulted in the deaths of 72 people and exposed systemic failures in building safety regulations, oversight and emergency response. The tragedy uncovered inadequate fire safety measures, substandard building materials and neglect of concerns raised by residents. Despite inquiries and recommendations for reforms to improve safety standards and hold accountable those responsible for the failures, progress has been slow.

Command and control, a hierarchical structure of decision making and coordination used by governments to manage disaster, follows a protocol of assessing and intervening but often leads to rigid, slow decision making, limited information flow, poor interagency coordination and a failure to engage communities and understand what people need. With the Grenfell disaster there was an outpouring of support and attention on social media offered by people with no connection to the situation – yet the government and housing provider were silent for days. What the assess–intervene–restructure approach lacks is humanity, care, an understanding of human needs and behaviour. This social pain sits in a context where the rich and the poor live within metres of each other and have very different whole life experiences. Data released in June 2017 by Trust for London and New Policy Institute shows large divides between rich and poor in the borough of Kensington and Chelsea. Wander around this small borough and you'll find Duke of York Square, a beautiful area with chic stores, galleries and artisan food. The local foodbank is a 15-minute walk away. Statistics show 29% of children in Kensington and Chelsea are living in poverty. It's a borough with the highest average incomes in London – and one of the highest deprivation scores in the capital city.

The government eventually set up a helpline for residents and survivors to help coordinate government support services and a fund was set up to help with living costs. Eight chaotic days after the event, an announcement by the Prime Minister stated in the House of Commons that anyone affected by the tragedy, regardless of their immigration status, would be entitled to support, including healthcare services and accommodation. These helplines and announcements aimed to fix people's situations one by one but didn't change the years of ignoring people's needs.

Plastic change

The Grenfell disaster highlights the need for mending and tending, rather than fixing and forgetting. In learning about pain and the human experience, we are starting to see just how possible change can be.

Neuroplasticity is the brain's ability to reorganize itself by forming new neural connections. This process allows the brain to adapt to changes in its environment, learn new information and recover from injury or trauma. Crumple, smooth and recrumple. There is compelling evidence that focusing on and encouraging neuroplasticity is a more successful way of treating chronic pain than structural medical fixing. A recent study found psychological treatment centred on changing patients' beliefs about the causes and threat value of pain may provide substantial and durable pain relief for people with chronic back pain. In a clinical trial by the University of Colorado, a survey demonstrated that 33 of 50 participants (66%) who had four weeks of pain reprocessing therapy were pain free, or nearly pain free, at post treatment, compared with 10 of 51 participants (20%) who were given a placebo and 5 of 50 participants (10%) who received the usual medical care. These benefits were still there one year after the intervention. Similar studies have found other chronic pain can be alleviated with these neuroplasticity-focused approaches.

Neuroplasticity-focused approaches for chronic pain management are 'whole life' approaches because they address not only the physical aspects of pain but also the psychological, emotional and social dimensions of the person's experience. Medical interventions are part of the solution alongside neuroplastic approaches. Some of these approaches are intermittent fasting, somatic movement, sensory therapies, Cognitive-Behavioural Therapy (CBT), arts practice, massage, community and lifestyle changes, biofeedback, nerve stimulation and many more whole life interventions.

To heal societal pain, a similar holistic approach is needed; whole life and whole system. Catastrophes cannot be understood or learned from by zoning in on one fail and pointing to the bit that made it happen. The responsibility and the healing needs to be held collectively. Scoring all the hurts, then fixing the ones with the highest score does not work for our pain-filled bodies or our pain-filled society. Just like neuroplasticity in our brains and bodies, social plasticity is the ability to reorganize society by forming new connections between our experience and a better future, adapting to changes in the environment, learning and healing from injury or trauma. Mending and tending.

⌣ Threshold: Why use Healing-Centred Design?

As we spend time with our pain, we notice what we need to mend and tend to – physically, emotionally and societally – and this causes emotion to rise up. Healing-Centred Design helps you channel the emotion into change-making work while tending to your own needs and nurturing healing.

Why use Healing-Centred Design?

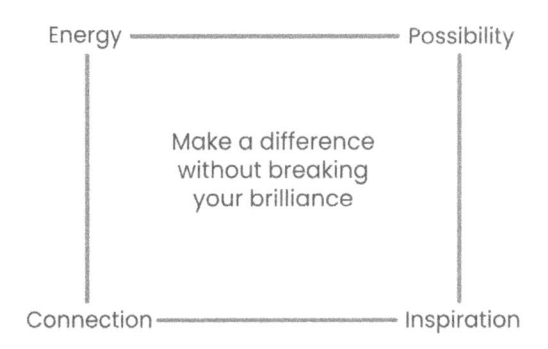

```
Energy ——————————— Possibility
          Make a difference
          without breaking
          your brilliance
Connection ——————————— Inspiration
```

> ### Case study: Gabz Pearson, co-founder of Menstrual Health Project
>
> Gabz Pearson is the co-founder (with Anna Cooper) of Menstrual Health Project, a UK charity supporting people who experience menstrual health conditions and concerns. They share educational toolkits in a digestible format, provide educational experiences in schools and workplaces and help people access medically accurate information about menstrual health.
>
> > Meeting Gabz was such a moment of recognition for me. She shared her personal and medical journey, and themes from my life were mirrored back to me, enriched with

her own understanding and raw experiences. There was a refreshing honesty to how she explained a difficult childhood, rejection, people pleasing and the challenges that came with unconventional thinking. She explained multiple interconnected health issues that she has had to join the dots around and the pain of battling broken systems for diagnosis, treatment and support.

Painsomnia?! I felt kindness extended out to me, in the early hours of the morning the day after I interviewed Gabz. I was awake. I was distracting myself from a (medically induced menopause) hot flush, with a little Instagram scrolling (I know, I know). A message pinged up, 'Are you awake too?' Gabz was online, in pain, and as we chatted I noticed how nice and easy it was to interact with someone in a way that allows things to just be. 'Hurting? That's shit, me too – here is a pic of my cute dog having a cuddle!'

She's a natural communicator and loves helping people, but Gabz and her work isn't all about peer support. There is a depth of knowledge that is inspiring. Menstrual Health Project has a Medical Advisory Board and works with people with lived experience to educate and gather data to influence policy makers. With the expertise of the board, they have created two toolkits to support menstrual health and wellbeing. These toolkits are full of accurate, digestible information on various aspects of menstrual health.

Gabz is not a gatekeeper. She speaks with lightness about her brilliant doctor and what she has learned from the online community, the power of the relationship with her co-founder Anna and the relief of working with someone who understands your pain. But she also speaks about qualitative and quantitative research, NICE (the National Institute for Health and Care Excellence in the UK) guidelines, medical pathways and HR governance, and busts myths and taboos in schools and workplaces in England and Wales.

'It's not like I'm waiting for a fridge freezer to be delivered – this is my health and life I'm waiting for!' Deftly using her personal experience to explain systemic problems, Gabz explained the frustrations of long waiting lists and disjointed medical pathways, sexism baked into medical professions and being let down by services, forcing her to become an angry advocate for her own needs. Double frustration means emotion-filled advocacy often has the knock-on effect, and professionals disengage or dismiss. Sometimes bringing hard medical facts, your own research or back-up people, to demonstrate you are not being unreasonable are the only things that work with doctors.

In our conversation, I was reminded that the emotional responses we express are not only valid but are also often vital to force the systems to take action. Annoyingly, one gynaecologist I had only took action when my husband came with me to the appointment, and I have asked (demanded sometimes) for the next pain management options only after I have done my own research to find out what these are. Gabz only heard about the pain reliever Vagus Nerve Stimulation (VNS), an implantable device which delivers electrical impulses to regulate inflammation responses, when her co-founder told her about it and she then told her doctor. Thanks to this information, she is awaiting trial for a spinal cord stimulator to ease her pain. I am now going to read up on this too!

When we need and want to create system change, it's a combination of evidence, lived experience, collaboration and influence that often moves the dial. We need people like Gabz and organizations like Gabz has set up – committed to changing things to create a better future for themselves and others. This is the clear cause that Menstrual Health Project exists for, and they are turning pain into power in educational and actionable ways every day.

Coincidentally, Gabz lives not far from my mum and sisters, so a coffee date is on the cards! I have a few buzzy ideas for collaborations and there is a clear link between her work and Healing-Centred Design. But for now I'm not going to gatekeep either. Go and visit Menstrual Health Project website. All genders and people can benefit from learning more about menstrual health and the charity is designed to be accessible, relevant and straightforward, infused with that honesty, kindness and knowledge that Gabz embodies.

https://menstrualhealthproject.org.uk/

◯ Reflective practice: Release it

What is it?

Releasing is about letting go. Through this chapter exploring pain, you may have built up some creative energy, tension or emotion. This activity provides a container in which to release your pent up thoughts or bubbling energy onto the page.

How do I do it?

Consider this story: A painter is asked to paint a mural in one day. He spends the morning sitting quietly, absorbing his surroundings and staring at the blank wall. In the afternoon he paints a wondrous vivid mural. An onlooker said, 'You had all day. Why did you only work in the afternoon?' The painter blinked in surprise, 'What do you mean?' he asks, 'I did all the work in the morning!' The morning with the blank wall is where the design, the planning, the preparation, the exploration of options and the choices happened.

Now it's your turn. Start with a blank page, write 'RELEASE' down the side and set a timer for ten minutes. Look out of a window or close your eyes, letting your mind wander through the challenges and possibilities ahead. Once the timer ends, reset it for another ten minutes. Return to your page and let your thoughts spill out – doodle, sketch or write. Use these prompts to guide you:

> **R**emedies: What helps when things are hard?
> **E**ase: How can you simplify and create ease?
> **A**lternatives: What have you tried, what could you try?
> **L**ight: Describe the light you are moving towards, how does it feel?
> **E**nergy: What activates you, what fires you up?
> **A**lign: Write down your needs and wants, notice overlaps and distinctions.
> **S**can: List the opportunities you can see.
> **E**xplore: What do you want to find out more about or immerse yourself in?

What next?

These notes are your 'Quest Notes' describing your beginnings and aspirations. Add them to your collection alongside your Invitation, nurturing them as you move forward.

2

Doorway two: Principles

A long corridor led you to this door, the walls holding memories. Passing through you feel echoes of emotion and experience. The door ahead is wooden, surrounded by an ornate gold frame, smaller than you imagined. The simple door exaggerates the expressive frame and the entrance feels both important and homely. A curved handle turned slowly, smoothly opens the door into the next space, a gallery with curated walls of images displayed. A voice you recognize, warm and loving, reads a poem to you as you step through the door.

Cast: A poem for shaping

Wax, on water
The light melts solidity into droplets, softening edges
Candle wax of time.

Flame, warming a pool
Wax relaxes, liquifies, escaping, rolling down the spine
Everything changes.

Fall, finding spherical form.
Concave leaves form instantly, hot wax meets cool water

Petaled shapes cast,
Fragile, floating, forming.

By Kerry Tottingham

Healing-centred principles

Pain, conditioning, pleasure, creativity and power are all experiences that form and reform us as we move through the melody of life experience. Along the way we collect truths, knowings, things we feel to be right in our bones. It's these deep knowings that help us form our principles and guiding values that make up the foundation of how we feel and experience. Principles are often forged in fire, going through flames to emerge with wisdom or malleable until plunged into an experience, like wax in water. The principles of Healing-Centred Design formed with the discovery that personal pain and societal pain are intertwined. Let me explain.

Have you had the experience of your body changing? Heavier or more muscular or more groomed or less flexible, in reaction to your environment, a relationship, the pressures on you or the time you have? These changes, often external changes, are expected and normalized. Most of us understand that stress might cause weight changes, self-esteem can influence how we take care of our bodies and our daily experiences and habits impact how our bodies feel and work.

So it's not too far a leap to say that societal pain might be linked to personal pain. Trauma is usually associated with physical or mental pain. But in a social context, trauma might show up as a population caught in emotional distress, mental health diagnosis ever increasing, extremism increasing or scarcity becoming normalized. Could the trauma of racism cause chronic fatigue? Could childhood poverty cause cancer? Could generational trauma cause diabetes? The answer is an emphatic yes. Trauma, threat, fear and helplessness are all connected to physical pain in well-researched and tangled ways. Societal pain, often experienced in childhood, may well be the root cause of much personal pain we face now. With this insight, you may have landed, like me, in a place of sickening acceptance that the medical profession is ill equipped to heal your pain. If the root cause is societal pain, no amount of pills or scans or operations will help.

But this is not the end of the story because adverse experiences causing future problems is not inevitable. Evidence shows that adverse childhood experiences (ACEs) can increase the risk of future health and behavioural issues, but this evidence also states that they *do not* guarantee such outcomes. Research indicates that resilience factors, such as supportive relationships and community resources, can mitigate the negative effects of ACEs. For instance, a study published in *BMC Public Health* found that community support and opportunities for development can build children's resilience, protecting them against some harmful impacts of ACEs.

Creating a system that mends the impact of pain and tends to our needs, to empower and create collective power that we can use to change the things that hurt us, is the purpose of Healing-Centred Design. An understanding of both the impact of trauma and the ways to mitigate it is essential to the design and justice work that follows. Post-traumatic growth emerged from studies exploring the positive psychological changes individuals can undergo after experiencing adversity or trauma. We can all relate to the phone call made by the passenger on a plane on course to crash, declaring their love, immortalized by film in our collective memories. Maybe we know people who have found purpose following a traumatic life event. Sometimes these shifts are sudden. For me, a long, expensive and slow process of therapy taught me how relational safety looked and felt. The post-traumatic growth I found on the other side of this feeling was a gentle and magical reacquainting with my imagination.

The company I founded, A Brilliant Thing CIC, works with community organizations and local authorities to understand how to become trauma-responsive places. We asked the question, 'How could the purpose-led sector prevent, protect and support people while mitigating trauma's consequences and developing a supportive place to live?' In 2023–2025, we worked with 100 organizations in Bolton, funded by the Bolton Council Public Health department, and collaborated with volunteers and people with lived experience of trauma, community organizations and statutory teams. We used design thinking (an approach described in the 'Process' section of this book) to co-create an accessible toolkit and support programme to develop trauma-informed ways of working that help everyone feel safe and supported. We were inspired by Dr Karen Treisman, a leading expert in trauma-informed care in the UK. Dr Treisman has authored several books and resources aimed at supporting children and families affected by trauma and we loved her accessible and illustrated textbooks such as *A Treasure Box for Creating Trauma-Informed Organizations: A Ready-to-Use Resource for Trauma, Adversity, and Culturally Informed, Infused and Responsive Systems,* which are rich with resources. The learning from this project, combined with our own lived experience and research, helped us to develop principles that support healing-centred development. These principles are the foundation of Healing-Centred Design and the cornerstone of how we operate as an organization.

Healing-Centred Design principles

- **Rhythm and ritual**: Practices and processes that create patterns and certainty.
- **Filter**: Clarity to help sort, prioritize and choose. What is okay? What is not okay?
- **Collide and align**: Bringing together ideas from different sources and blending to create something new; this widens perspective and creates opportunity for new thinking.
- **Transition**: The spaces in between the action. Creating pauses for processing, making connections and reflection.
- **Contribute and benefit**: Noticing the relationship between giving with receiving and adjusting as needed.

These principles have helped us grow and develop, framed projects and programmes, and are the backbone of our communication. You might notice these principles shaping how this book is organized and how we communicate publicly. They are so adaptable because they are organized around human needs for certainty, choice, difference, reflection and community. They also chime with the six principles of trauma-informed care outlined by the UK Government Office for Health Improvement and Disparities: safety, choice, collaboration, trust, empowerment and cultural consideration. Our healing-centred principles work externally to create and deliver powerful work in healing-centred ways, but they also work internally and can be used to heal relationships and support self-development. Let's explore each in turn.

Rhythm and ritual

You might associate these words with music and religion, or seasons and routines. They are words that speak of beginnings, endings and patterns. Rhythms and rituals are especially important when we feel chaos or lack of control. For example, a missed alarm and panicked wake-up is eased with the knowledge that Mondays always begin with meeting the same person at the same time. Rhythms and rituals create safety; we know and trust in what's coming next. I'll share some of the rhythms and rituals of my life so you can start making these words personal.

The rhythm of my pain has been hard to catch. It repeats in a cycle but I can't track it exactly; it clusters and blooms, eases and comes back. My life rhythms have been similar, intense periods of action, open spaces of searching and wandering. The intense periods are where I am alive, creative, focused and connected. People are there and energy, so much inspiring energy.

The fallow stretches have become rarer, the busyness has crowded in, chasing the energy and expansion. But I remember these expanses of time; the eight-hour delayed train journey where I changed the course of my life with a notebook. The ritual solo trips to London and Brighton, wandering the streets and following my nose down quiet roads that lead to treasure troves. The edges of places, the gritty parts, artists' houses, perfect views captured in my grainy analogue camera. The realizations and discoveries found in big sweeps of time where no one knew where I was.

In these extended moments, I felt uncomfortable, painful even to be alone and purposeless, roaming around in a place or in my mind. But I notice this yearning now for emptiness and the fallow that precedes the fertile. I wonder if my pain is meeting my yearning: if pain is yearning; if the pain of abuse is the yearning for respect; if the pain of scarcity is the yearning for enough; if the pain of oppression is yearning for freedom.

I know that these rhythms of action and inaction have been important in my life, and seen with hindsight, these solo quests have been rituals that moved me from one place to another. Noticing existing rhythms and rituals gives insight into the ways this principle might support change.

In music, rhythm is the foundational element that gives a piece its flow. It's the pattern of strong and weak beats that create the pulse, and the tempo that sets the pace. Rhythm is the framework that organizes musical phrases and sections, bringing together notes, instruments and voice in complexity. Rhythm is what makes you tap your foot, nod your head or sway to the music – rhythm is an expression.

In life, rhythm provides a similar beat – a pulse that flows through everything: your steps as you walk; the rise and fall of your breath; the ebb and flow of the sea. It's the pattern of days and nights, the seasons changing, the cycles of birth and death and the moon. Creating rhythms in our day, week and year or within projects and communities helps create the patterns that our human brain loves.

In our organization we use the language of rhythms to describe habits and regular moments. We have a rhythm of weekly priority setting, communication rhythms between team members and project management rhythms. These are all crafted and designed with healing in mind. For example, within our weekly priority setting, each team member sets a number of priorities that correlate to the number of days they work, so if you work three days, you can have three priorities. This means we have to be discerning and hold our own boundaries around time, expectation and output, creating a way of working that aligns with our healing-centred approach.

What's the difference between rhythms and rituals?

When teaching these principles I often get asked this question. I most often reflect it back to the group as I believe we all have some inner knowledge in response to this question. Here are some of the answers I have heard:

- In the kitchen, a ritual means putting the music on, getting your knives ready, cooking then cleaning and clearing the space as the dish cooks. The rhythm is about how you move between tasks.
- Following a set routine, a ritual guides your day, while rhythm sets the pace, keeping you in motion.
- Ritual is preparation, rhythm is sensation.
- In yoga, rituals shape your practice, while rhythm syncs breath and movement.

- Before performing, rituals give me a routine. If I am late and cannot warm up I worry I'll ruin the performance. But in the moment on the stage, rhythm is always there to carry you through.
- It makes me think of a garden. Rituals mark the seasons, like the ritual of preparing the garden for winter, then weeding and watering are rhythms that help everything grow.
- In my culture, rituals provide community structure and are connected to religion and also the human experiences of birth, death and coming of age. Maybe the rhythms are the daily habits like prayer that deepen the spiritual experience and keep you connected.
- Work meetings follow rituals, providing structure and order, while rhythm is the tasks that create movement and progress.
- Creative rituals help me get inspired. At the start of projects I spend time gathering inspiration, photos, examples of other artists' work and source materials then, when in the project, rhythm is coming back to these things regularly to keep the work flowing.

You can see from these many different examples that in most cases the context provided some kind of container. People could think of examples of rituals and rhythms in relation to a particular role or circumstance. The ritual examples involve a set of actions often with a start, middle and end. They are often repeated at significant times and provide both structure and a sense of connection, meaning or continuity. Rituals may also involve symbolic gestures, traditions or ceremonies that hold personal or cultural significance, meaning they are important practices that contribute to a sense of identity, belonging or fulfilment.

Rituals can be simple or complex, involve others or be experienced solo. You can craft beautiful rituals to celebrate or design a ritual to mark an ending. Morning or bedtime rituals can have a profound impact on how we experience our day. Rituals around setting up a community project can set the tone and encourage engagement from the start. The garden ritual looks after the plants and earth long into the winter. Rituals create memories and can both prepare and reflect. They have lasting impacts.

Rhythms are patterned flow or regular recurrence tasks, actions or other elements. Rhythm creates momentum in activities and experiences, connecting the dots between rituals and outcomes. You can think of rhythms as simple habits, regular repetitions that over time become effortless and automatic, sometimes flexing and adapting to change and influencing the experience for you and others.

Rhythms and rituals help us have a sense of control. For people experiencing pain of any type having some certainty and feeling of control can be an antidote to hopelessness. Of course creating rigidity within this, overly controlling our experience can be damaging too, which is why the language of rhythms and rituals, and their connections to music, spirituality and creative expression, are so useful.

Filter

This principle can seem quite shouty at first; it speaks of rules to filter in and filter out.

Filter! Trust your gut! Use the data! Lead by example! Surround yourself with who you want to be! So much advice, mostly unsolicited, blaring in words and images, shouting through screens, blare… blare… blare, without noticing who is watching.

But 'filter' is an organizing principle. It helps us decide, choose and focus. When we want clarity, filter helps us sort and prioritize.

How do I decide?

How do I know what's okay and what's not okay? I'm quite impulsive. I say yes to potential, momentarily checking in with myself to see how I feel, and often it's excitement that drives my yes. But I have sturdy boundaries. I don't go to meetings when an email is enough or get someone else out of thinking for themselves. I am intentional about where I spend my time and energy. If pockets open in my day, I know who I want to have a meaningful connection with. I'm great at time blocking and delegating – mostly!

But filter still challenges me. A boundary can feel like steel in the daytime, but at night as the light shifts, the steel wall becomes tinfoil and pain punches through. Without the distracting, immersive joy of potential filled work or energy of a group, I often fade in the evening. Cocooned by a blanket and hot water bottle, wiped out by the pain that now erupts or the effort of keeping it at bay.

Steely, still?

Maybe my filter needs to be made of a different material if this metal isn't working for me. Maybe it could be silk, woven in fine strands, stronger than steel, but flexible, lightweight and breathable. Silk wrapping and draping through my day, letting air in, protecting and shaping. A silk filter changes shape depending on what's beneath it, sheathing decisions, actions and emotions with a layer of care. Maybe that meeting might be worthwhile, that connection I crave might be damaging, that exciting idea might need tempering or passing along to another. The silk filter doesn't have hard edges that crumple under pressure. The silk filter adapts and lets me choose again each time.

We all need a filter system. Often in my work I help groups design and develop decision-making processes. These processes then become the filter through which projects flow, removing things that do not align with their purpose or vision or don't move them towards their desired outcome. This is tender work. People can be very attached to their beliefs about what is right or wrong, correct or off course. I always begin by exploring different decision-making models with the group, explaining different models, allowing time for personal reflection then a facilitated discussion surfaces where the group has commonality and where there is difference. The group may lean towards hierarchical decision making or need quality data before decisions are made. Some people may prefer consent or consensus; consent focuses on individual autonomy and agency (everyone says yes) while consensus focuses on collaboration and mutual understanding to achieve a shared objective (no one says no).

Sometimes we explore the circles of tolerance, drawing concentric circles on big pieces of paper. The centre circle is labelled 'Yes', the next, 'I can live with it', the next 'Not sure', the next 'Feeling uncomfortable' and the last circle is labelled 'Hell no!' Beginning with some fun scenarios, list 'Eat at a vegan restaurant' or 'Go to a Taylor Swift concert', then people can map where they would place themselves on the scale. We can then change an element of the scenario, 'A vegan restaurant with your best friend' and see how people's positions change. Then we can move onto exploring decision making at work and use the circles to have useful conversations about why conflict occurs and different people's expectations and understandings.

These workshops usually lead to the development of a flow chart or model to help the group at decision-making points; co-created they are more likely to work. The first few times the models are used, steady facilitation is needed as people often revert back to decision-making styles they have been conditioned with or that feel most comfortable. It takes time to form habits around filtering, and our rhythm and ritual principle comes in handy here too.

However, you create your own filter, as simply as two lists titled 'Okay' and 'Not okay' or as involved as a co-produced decision-making model, knowing your filter can help you make choices that feel aligned with who you are, what you need and where you are going.

Collide and align

This one I love – I'm an idea junkie. Collide and align is about blending ideas from different places to create something new. It's also about diversity, cultural considerations and recognizing and valuing difference. Colliding can create energy, sometimes dissent and challenging. Aligning creates harmony, enabling difference to exist together. Dissent and repair is a normal part of group work and often is the birthplace of innovation. We need to both actively bring in colliding ideas, people, differences and work *and* align and blend if we want to create new things. When you are bored, stuck or feel disconnected, this principle is a brilliant way to get things moving.

Art making is a great way to practise colliding and aligning. Finding and choosing different, opposing colours or materials and combining to create a cohesive artwork. I have an image I call to mind of a woman in a cloak wandering through woods and shorelines, gathering shells, moss and fallen leaves that curl in interesting ways, evoking the shape of the land. She gathers from different places, her sack an eclectic collection of found objects: a feather, a rock, a twist of metal. She sees the way the light glimmers on seafoam water, in the gleam of a waxy leaf and in the steam rising from sun-soaked fields. Pausing, she places the soft moss next to a yellow petal, crowned with a foil sweet wrapper. The yellow glows and the layered, curling edges of the moss are defined on the shiny paper, green and distinct in a way that the forest floor could not show. I love thinking of and making these types of assemblages; three-dimensional, small artworks combining found objects and materials to make compositions. I'm inspired by Joseph Cornell, a shy artist who created poetic, surreal assemblages within boxes. I especially love finding ways to create visual relationships between seemingly disparate parts, folding different textured fabrics into repeated shapes or shaping a harmonious sentence from words cut from different pages.

I could disappear into this daydream for days. In fact, my work often has this feel. I've designed a company around these questions:

- What would happen if we placed that with this, combined art and science, community and enterprise – what would align or separate?
- Could we bring things together in ways that are meaningful, powerful and poetic?
- What emotion is evoked?
- What can be learned from contrasts?
- Can art emerge from disparate parts brought together with care?

Collide and align is about surfacing diversity. What are all the potentials, ideas, stories and experiences we can gather? How can we take ideas from different places and blend to create something new?

Transition

Transition, transient, transformation. Passing, passage, past and present. What happens in between things? Transition is about pausing, resting, reflecting and moving through. Transition also means letting go of what you don't need any more and opening up to what you might need next. It's a useful principle when you are seeking wisdom and nurturing your own intuition.

My mum's counselling business was called 'Transitions'. When my sisters and I had stopped playing in the garden and we were too tall to create imaginary worlds in the shady undergrowth, I remember her summerhouse office being built. Tucked away at the back of the garden, with a separate entrance and stone path laid down, it felt like a real version of our childhood fairy houses made of leaves. Dappled in light this was where she saw clients, a world which we were not part of, easing people through their changes and losses, transitions and emotions. She had a sign made in slate, the word 'Transitions' carved into its surface. I see this carved sign when I am sitting with change, options laid out, and I imagine running my fingers over the carved script; a comforting, rhythmic action.

Once, when navigating a tricky part of life, I was gifted a wisp of advice. It's a gem I've carried with me and practised often through the beginnings and completions and ebbs and flows of experience. 'Maybe you should just walk through the door.' It was said with such ease, such freedom. Because I felt trapped at the time, it seemed like such a simple solution that could not be that easy. Later that day the words floated past me again and I caught them with the urgency of a flame curling around dry tinder. Feeling a bit stupid, I got up and considered the door between the living room and stairs. I noticed a splash of coffee I hadn't wiped and heard the quiet screech of the hinge that needed some attention; this wasn't the door. The kitchen door wasn't the one either, with its monotony of cooking and cleaning on the other side in a room I'd fallen out of love with. I instinctively needed a door with a clunk – heavier, and the close more final.

I walked over to the front door, eased it open and practised stepping in and out. As my mind searched for a reason and felt a bit silly, my body understood the symbolism. On one side of the door was sadness, clutter and pain. On the other side was a slightly wild garden with hopeful planting nestled in between a tangle of ivy and an overgrown hydrangea. As I moved in and out, I noticed the hollyhocks were struggling, but I was encouraged by the heavy bloom of blue hydrangea pom poms beaconing me to come into the garden. It was a hot, dry day. I closed the black door behind me and lent backwards, the hot shiny black paint warming my back. Dust from the road and a neighbour's summer bonfire was trapped in shards of light, scenting the air with woody mist. I breathed in deeply and looked around. This was the moment I decided to move, make change, transform things.

Sometimes we can create the environment we need for transition – small tasks or routines or physical changes to signal a movement and set our brains and bodies up for it. For example, in between waking and getting up I read my horoscope, in between work and home I pack up my co-working space: my orange insulated mug, heated seat pad, sticker covered laptop, green ink pen, notebook and meds pouch. These things I set out and pack up, set out and pack up. The range of inky pens, green like my mum uses, and a sky blue and a maroon. Sometimes I pick up the red one by mistake and all day I feel like I'm marking work. Sometimes the black ink flows like relief and order. The notebooks I keep buying and filling, buying and filling, even when typed notes would be more efficient. Its soft, fake leather cover and off-white pages help me focus and remember. Objects are important markers when working with transition. I think of them as talismans.

A talisman is an object for luck, magic, representing safe passage or symbols of hope. Transient moments, pauses in between, are stifled in our working-from-home make-every-moment-count lives. Podcasts while driving, 8am phone calls to doctors interrupting breakfast, maximizing diaries with AI to fit in as much as possible. Maybe our pauses need talismans? Physical objects to remind us about the importance of the transition. Combined with rituals, the setting out and packing away of everyday objects that hold meaning and purpose – and maybe some magic.

(As I have mentioned!) I hate the idea of pacing. Pacing is a technique often advised for long-term or chronic pain management. It involves doing a low level of activity throughout the day, maintaining an even level of energy and avoiding the crash and burn cycle. In principle this sounds great, but our bodies are not machines. A sewing machine will last longer and work better if it is used moderately and consistently every day rather than sewing like a demon one day then being left in a cupboard for months. But a human body is not a machine – it works in rhythms, cycles. I have more energy at different times of the day, week and month. Sometimes inspiration fires up and infuses me with the flow that keeps me creating. Sometimes I need to stop for a block of time, those fallow periods. Maintaining a consistent baseline of activity goes against our nature.

A regular practice of pausing, however, I can get on board with. Checking in with myself about my activity and energy, asking what's driving it: fear or love, creativity or scarcity, keeping up or flowing forward. And because a pause, a check-in, is the most easily cut thing when time is short or days are busy, ascribing meaning to objects as reminders to take these pauses could be a smart (and pain relieving) way of keeping these vital spaces in between safe. When I worked in the charity sector, where those everyday moments of replenishing are hard to find, I learned to think about 'filling up' in a new way. I found it easier and more fulfilling to dedicate a week to filling up. For those of us who work best in a 'project' kind of way, or hate task-switching, it feels more natural to allocate a block of intentional time for pausing.

There are seven types of rest. Recently, I wanted to explore new ways to pause and transition between moments of action. As a starting point, I listed the seven types of rest:

- Physical
- Mental
- Spiritual
- Emotional
- Sensory
- Creative
- Social

I chose to intentionally 'do' each type and post about my experiences online.

Highs and lows

Days one and two felt clunky, like I was shoehorning rest into my diary like another 'to-do'. I was getting up earlier to fit in rest, which when you write it down seems slightly counter intuitive! I'd booked a massage, and though it was lovely, I left feeling frustrated with my body and for not speaking up when my back hurt. I noticed I was attaching a lot of expectation to this week of rest.

During days three and four I noticed I was slowing down, becoming quieter and more focused. This meant I was completing other tasks in less time, giving more time up for rest. I took two afternoons off to spend with the kids.

One of these was a gorgeous sunny day and we went into Manchester. This wasn't my choice, but the kids are at that age when shopping is a thing! I was slightly nervous that my sensory and emotional rest would be scuppered by hot dog stands, street hustle and blaring 'buy me' displays. But I felt an odd sense of calm strolling through town, reflecting with the kids that when they were younger everything was dictated by the routine of meals, bedtimes and managing their needs, and how it feels easier now and we forget about time a little bit.

On day five I had a wobble. Grey, rain-soaked views dampened my mood and I spent the morning hiding from this challenge. I had thought it was 'creative rest' day and my imagination was sluggish. I realized the attachment I have to making and creating and the tension between making 'art' and using creativity to rest – I didn't want to make and show something that wasn't 'good'. Then I realized it was actually 'sensory rest' day! Relief washed over me, I had permission to hunker down, be quiet and limit sensory input. The day unfolded slowly and calmly.

On day six I woke full of beans, despite a broken night's sleep (I spent two hours in the bath with endo/bladder pain, finishing my book and using my imagination to reflect on it – a great pain reliever!). The creative rest time on this day felt possible and playful. I sorted boxes of art materials and played with some ideas. In the evening, I'd booked a pottery class with my husband. I did ceramics at A-Level, and it felt so good to get my hands on some clay again! This eased me into day seven's 'social rest', which I used to focus on meaningful relationships, turning off the socials and settling into family time.

Reflections

Reflecting on expectations, anticipations, needs and hopes is a useful way to start the week. I did this mid-week and from that point I felt more connected and committed to the experience and was able to let go a little bit. I needed my own fill-your-cup coaching session before starting the next week of rest! The weather, my surroundings and other sensory inputs really affect my experiences. A messy, chaotic space ramps up my stress. It helps when I express these experiences and ask for help to change the space when it's possible. You might find that colour or sound or smells or light have more of an impact on you when you are stressed – focus on ways to regulate yourself if you can't change the environment.

Creativity is my comfort zone, but I hold lots of fear around this too: getting it right and validation. It may be that a type of rest feels risky to you. Bringing awareness to the risk helps to move through it.

Contribute and benefit

Contribute and benefit is a principle that helps us create community and connection around our lives and the purpose-led work we are doing. It's both giving and receiving that creates the web of community and the bonds of connection. If we give and never receive, we burn out. If we benefit and never contribute, we either become passive and disempowered, or dismissive and entitled. So often in purpose-led work we over-prioritize giving and forget about receiving. Sometimes we can give more, other times less, but knowing both are needed helps create change in sustainable ways.

Healing-Centred Design is a container for this change. A container that is generously curved, safely receiving what is given to us and offering what we can contribute out to the work. Holding and supporting multiplicities of emotions and ideas like the ingredients of flour, yeast, sugar and water, mixing together to rise up.

Contribution, giving time and energy to others, only really lands with the intention it is given if it also comes with a balance of benefit. If I over-give without replenishing myself, I will burn out or begin to resent you. Some people can give more while receiving less because their cups are already full. Equity means that if I have more money, I could pay for my meal and my friend's meal. She might have less money but gives her valuable time to help me work out a problem over dinner. We are both able to give and receive in ways that reflect our situational differences. There is a cleanness to mutual contribution and benefit.

Recently, I delivered a presentation, discussing the concept of systemic change, network building and the importance of engagement. To a slightly bemused zoom room who are used to presentations about data and intelligence, I described a murmuration or flock of starlings moving together in a swirling drift. I explained how the flock was not one group but multiple seven-bird groups. Each seven overlaps with another seven, which overlaps with another, forming a networked system that together protects and provides opportunities for the flock.

I remember how captivated I had been when I learned about this concept in Adrienne Maree Brown's book *Emergent Strategy*. The murmuration behaves as a critical system, poised to respond in an instant to environmental changes, moving in formation. The birds don't bump into each other, they don't have a leader and they don't disperse. They follow some rules of engagement:

- **Separation**: Nearby birds move further apart, giving each other space.
- **Cohesion**: Distant birds move closer together, providing connection.
- **Alignment**: Birds align their direction and fly with each other.

The flock thrives when each bird contributes and each bird benefits. Contribute and benefit is an important principle in change work because many of us in the purpose-led space form a flock of over-givers. We are conditioned to give and judge receiving, which ultimately will damage the whole flock. Remembering this risk when organizing means we can set up projects and work in ways that make space for giving but also receiving. This might ebb and flow depending on your starting point, your needs and your privilege, but we all do have needs to be met, desires to be fulfilled and plenty to offer each other.

As we move forward, let's imagine birds taking flight, weaving and swirling with potential, watch them murmurate and let's consider who we can murmurate with too.

⌣ Threshold: How do the principles work?

The Healing-Centred Design principles were shaped by people who have experienced trauma and injustice. They draw on trauma-informed practice principles used in the NHS and healthcare settings, blend creative coaching principles and psychology around human needs.

But what matters most is they feel deeply nourishing, supportive and healing to use. The power they create transforms experiences in personal, team, organizational, community and societal development work.

How do the principles work?

This principle	helps you	create power
Rhythm + Ritual	Begin, end + create patterns	Safety
Filter	Sort, prioritise + choose	Clarity
Collide and Align	Blend difference + create new things	Innovation
Transition	Move, pause + reflect	Wisdom
Contribute + benefit	Balance giving + receiving	Community

Case study: Michael Weetman, founder of Roll to Recovery

Michael Weetman, founder of Roll to Recovery, combines his lived experience with his submission grappling (type of combat sport and martial art) to support people in substance misuse recovery, to rebuild resilience, connection and mental wellbeing.

In our conversation, Michael shared his experience of a complete perspective shift, one that he continues to stay close to and gave me a glimpse into a place where both hurt and hope live. It started as an illusion, then evolved into a deep trust.

> Michael has experienced many changes, entering and leaving the armed forces, fatherhood, changes in work and purpose. Some changes were actively pursued, others were consequences of his actions, or caused by the pull of compulsion. But the one that I was left thinking about after our conversation was the transformative move from impulse to choice. Setting up Roll to Recovery, an organization created to help people in recovery using the art of submission grappling, was an intentional and powerful choice he made to turn his own experience into a way of supporting others.
>
> Michael attended an Alcoholics Anonymous meeting feeling both powerless to choose and certain of his own strength to win the game of recovery — pride and ego hiding fragility. He heard someone else speak out the words that described his own inner narration. In that moment of recognition, hearing words

expressing exactly how he was feeling yet coming out of another's mouth, he thought it was a set-up. Something drew him in though. He kept attending and on the other side of disbelief and dismissal he eventually discovered a daily hope, faith and trust. This showed up in big life-changing ways, small life-affirming ways, becoming sober, having the ability to say sorry and finding ways that mend things.

Reactions, impulses, split second actions. This way of living was stressful, control filled, driven by fear. Keeping people and situations apart to ensure they could be controlled, compartmentalizing until those boxes exploded with dangerous and powerful energy. Explosions always harming him; damage to others was unintended but inevitable collateral. This way of living sounds so far from how Michael now describes how he experiences power these days.

In physics, an impulse is the change in momentum that happens when a force is applied over a specific time. Impulses are fast, without much time for consideration or discernment. In contrast, making intentional choices in response to a stimulus gives space to feel those impulsive urges and use them as information. Instincts are noticed, validated and listened to but not always acted on. Michael describes a progress bar, like you might see in a video game. Impulsive actions make the countdown speed up. Intentional choices slow everything down, offer time to think, make that window of time bigger so he can reflect, try and choose. Choice is one of the central trauma-informed principles reflected in 'Filter', the second of our Healing-Centred Design principles.

The past version of Michael was ambitious despite others, tangled up with fear and shame. Now he lives ambitiously with respect for himself and others. He knows creating space around his actions, taking time at the beginning of each day to reflect on how things honestly are rather than on how he wants them to be, is something he will always need to be conscious of. He recognizes his default reactions need tending, to protect the things he values inside himself and around him.

When we had this conversation, Michael was emerging from a difficult personal time, where he'd grappled with 'past him', feeling the depths of detachment, and he admitted that he hadn't wanted to speak that day. I'm glad he did though. We were both reminded that focusing on staying regulated and present, open and vulnerable, opens the door to trust,

> hope and possibility. The power in the internal and everyday processes is as valuable as the outcome itself. Michael signed off with a smile and shared, 'We can all be the work in progress and the masterpiece at the same time.'
>
> www.instagram.com/mwtrainingsystems/

◯ Reflective practice: Design it in

What is it?

Designing is about weaving imagination and action together. Designing is a playful way to encourage you to think audaciously about the change you wish to create, powered by trust, hope and possibility. Before you dive into designing transformation, practise using this technique to build your imagination muscle!

How do I do it?

Imagine designing a machine to bring your dreams to life. Have a play and think beyond the ordinary – who says this machine can't be powered by magic? Gather a pile of magazines and flick through them. Cut or tear out images and words inspired by the prompts below and use them to collate and design your 'Dream Collage'. Move your images around until you have a pleasing composition, then fix with glue or tape:

- **Ingredients**: What are the raw materials you have?
- **Wheels**: What helps things stay in motion?
- **Levers**: What mechanism pivots, lifts or moves things along?
- **Momentum**: What energy drives, pushes, pulls?
- **Mixer**: How can you blend, stir, combine and agitate?
- **Temperature**: What is hot, cold, frosty or bubbling?

What next?

You can use this Dream Collage to identify how the Healing-Centred Design principles might work for you. Consider:

- What is your collage telling you?
- Is it inspired by lots of different ingredients?
- Does a state change speak to you?
- Have you focused on the processes for mixing, combining or moving?
- How playful do you feel?

Your collection now includes your Invitation, Quest Notes and Dream Collage. Each piece is a reminder of your creativity and resolve.

3

Doorway three: Process

Behind this door there is rhythmic clunking and gentle taps, aromas drift out sweetly and you feel the energy of ideas bursting. The process room is where we craft and design ways to turn ideas into action, pain into power.

A large set of double doors open into a room full of light, multiple tools are arranged on one wall, wide benches for creating and experimenting. Big sheets of crisp, white paper and a rainbow of marker pens invite you in to explore and learn. The words of this poem are painted on the windows in tones staining the glass, shining coloured shapes across the room.

Vivid: A poem for making

Pristine contrast.
Billowy lilac storm seared with hummingbird yellow.
Paper paint, wet glow.
Moment cries, vivid, as fleeting perfection.

Handmade motion.
A wash of painty daydreams, blending liquid waterpot.
Water brush, swirling thought.
Colours bruise, mixing, as rememberings stir.

Melding future.
A path in moody pastels, rose flush, tawny green.
Fawny plum, tinged citrine.
Illustrated ways, just made, as foot touches.

By Kerry Tottingham

Healing-centred process

The word 'process' means a series of actions or steps taken to achieve a particular result or outcome. It involves systematic and organized activities that are carried out in a sequential or iterative way to achieve a specific goal. But this description doesn't capture the magic or power that a process can create!

The original idea for this book was to create a collection of the processes we use to organize and build in communities and call it 'Dream Scaffolding'. Scaffolding is a useful metaphor to describe how processes give change work structure while also supporting and shaping dreams. Processes are essential and when we connect them to our purpose and make them adaptable, they don't have to be rigid or repetitive. If purposeful direction, momentum or impact matters, having strength within your processes can make these things happen.

Healing-centred processes are designed to support the creation of the change and support the people doing the change work, as well as the people who will benefit from the change you are creating. The good news is that traditional processes can be tweaked to be more healing-centred, usually by seeing the process from multiple perspectives then refining and adjusting based on the core needs, supporting needs and desires of all involved.

For example, a hierarchical decision-making process might be adjusted to be healing-centred through thoughtful and transparent communication of what's happening at each stage of decision making, or by shifting where the decision takes place and who is involved. Often people have never considered how they make decisions together and on reflection realize different people are doing it in different ways and that is why a conflict keeps occurring. Common ways people identify are decisions based on gut reaction, quality of information, who benefits, time, money, the greater good or to make a point! Try having the conversation with your partner or a friend and exploring what influences their decision making. You might be surprised about what motivates them to make choices and decisions.

Processes like decision making often involve planning, organizing, learning and evaluation. We find learning about different frameworks, theories and approaches useful to help us build processes at A Brilliant Thing CIC and we love a diagram! Some of our favourites are participatory methods and co-production, systemic and design thinking, and coaching frameworks. Our processes are always crafted around our Healing-Centred Design principles.

Here are 20 processes that can be used to create change. Let the words inspire you or research the processes behind them to identify ways to strengthen the processes you use in your life and purpose-led work:

1. Habit formation
2. Goal setting
3. Storytelling
4. Restorative justice

5. Direct action steps
6. Learning programmes
7. Decision-making process
8. Change management process
9. Self-reflection routine
10. Co-production
11. Strategic planning process
12. Community-based participatory research
13. Problem-solving process
14. Training pathways
15. Idea generation process
16. Project management
17. Resilience building exercises
18. Self-care rituals
19. Recipes for change
20. Product development

The processes we find most useful in our work, and I find most useful in my life, are decision-making processes, relationship building systems, processes around money and time management, scheduling mechanisms and recipes (not just for food related creations!). The processes you need to create your dreams will depend on your needs and desires, but the methods described in this chapter are great starting points. Spend some time with some big paper mapping out your work and identifying what processes help you make things happen – are there ways you can centre healing within them?

A frame to dance within

A home is made within the structure of a house, though it's so much more than walls and floors. To create a home for transformation, we need a frame to dance within. Some structure, parameters, context and an edge to push. In therapy, a frame refers to the structure, boundaries and context that the therapist establishes to create a safe and effective therapeutic environment. The frame helps maintain consistency, trust and clarity in the therapeutic relationship. When working in ways that place healing at the centre of our own personal development or in purpose-led work, our dreams need a frame based on our values.

Back in my artist-in-residence days, I worked in a primary school in south Manchester. On different days I taught children from age 4 to 12, creating art in groups, connected to their topics and introducing them to materials; from willow weaving to felting, paper making to junk art. This role was the head teacher's clever plan. With art removed from the curriculum and teachers expected to teach art through science, maths and history, she noticed the children were not getting the creative play time, especially as they got older. She knew that art, creativity and group making helped with problem- solving to collaboration, relationship forming to experimentation.

So through a friend of a friend I was brought in to teach the teachers some creative skills through weekly arts sessions with the children, and afterschool enrichment sessions with families and teachers. It was a strange time in my life with a fairly new arrangement. For half the week I worked for a charity, coordinating arts projects and community events. In this half of the week my children lived with me, so school runs, washing and spellings over breakfast occupied my mind. In the other half of the week, the children lived with their dad, and I was an artist. I did jobbing artist work, random workshops, community centre projects and my own sketch booking (more for therapy than art). I relished the reduced responsibility and pined for the daily structure of mothering at the same time. Luckily, I was busy and surrounded by children in my role as artist-in-residence in the primary school, which helped with the missing of my own children. I learned as much as the school children in that time.

This frame to my week gave me space to occupy two roles – slightly disjointed, but with a clear Wednesday handover, mother to artist. The mother frame kept me grounded. I couldn't go off on whimsical or wild adventures for too long. The artist kept my inspiration alive. I could use my imagination then be back for Saturday handover. Though the disconnected way my life was operating at the time was not sustainable or something I wanted forever. During this time when my life had taken a new shape, the frame kept me steady.

On a rainy Friday morning in October, I was working in the school and planning to explore line and colour with Year 4. The school wanted me to work in double-page spreads, looking at artists and copying techniques, just as I had been taught in school. In my planning meeting with the teacher, I'd suggested a more relaxed approach, asking the children what they wanted to create. She'd looked alarmed. What if we don't have the materials? How can we help 30 children do different projects? What if they ask how to do something and I don't know? So we had agreed on more structure with a little experimenting with materials to start us off.

The teacher began, 'Don't ruin the first page, write your name and class neatly on the second page and underline it.' I sat quietly and watched some of the children fidget and disengage, staring at raindrops slithering down the window. Some of the clean sketchbooks became grubby with rubbed out wonky lines and pencil smudges. This classroom ritual seemed to take ages as the right pencils were found, sharpened and ruler sword fights were stopped. I noticed some of the girls take great pride in their neat letters and looking expectantly up for praise. A boy to my right cupped his hand around his words and I wondered why he didn't want me to see.

In those moments I felt the conditioning of school, oppressive and judgemental, pouring down as if the rainclouds were inside. Expression might ruin something, neat is good, erase what you get wrong, hide your imperfections. As the teacher handed over to me with an enthusiastic 'Miss is going to show you how to be an artist', I was thinking of Keri Smith's book, *Wreck the Journal*, which is a book full of creative prompts or 'destructive' acts – scratching surfaces, scribbling, painting with coffee, to experience the true creative process.

Instead of neat titles, we began by making background and borders. The challenge was to make as many backgrounds and borders as possible in that pristine sketchbook. I showed them how to dribble watercolour, paint water over felt tip to make it bleed, wax resist with crayons and use the wrong end of a pencil to make marks. It was messy, playful and led to what the children titled 'happy accidents' – unexpected marks, colours, surfaces and shapes.

Some children took a while to let go, worrying about getting it right. Others enthusiastically splashed and soaked pages until the teacher looked worried. They really had wrecked the book.

But the magic happened in the next week's lesson. Having been left to dry with strategic pens between the pages so they didn't stick, then with a heavy stack of books on top to flatten out the pages, the sketchbooks were transformed. They were not white pages but textured, patterned and toned surfaces, washes of colour absorbed into the page, ready to be written and drawn on. The backgrounds adding depth to the artwork we were now creating on top, borders sharpening up collages and inspiring line drawings within them.

By taking time to create backgrounds and borders, we had created a frame to dance within. By adapting the intimidating white pages, we had unlocked the creativity to play. The children had explored the edges and plains, the possibilities of materials and the differences between chalk, oil pastel and paints. The work we were now doing in the books, on top of and framed by the pre-work, flowed more easily and with more style and interest than a blank page could ever inspire. Maybe we had even created some alternatives to the conditioning the children were absorbing.

I've taken this 'frame to dance within' idea with me outside of school into project management, organizational development, communities and boardrooms. When creating anything new, parameters and context help. The frame might include timescales, budgets, expectations, commitments and anything fixed or certain (as can be!). There can be some creativity here, some testing of assumptions, stretching and pushing of the boundaries, but ultimately, we need a clear frame that everyone can see and trust in, creating a border for the work.

We also need a background. Who are the people involved? What is the economic, environmental, cultural, social or structural context? What is the history and potential here? Understanding of backgrounds takes time. Sometimes melding elements of the context together can create new context for the work. Bringing together a group of mixed-age people, within an area to interact with the surroundings, might give us a new context to design from, considering accessibility and function in new ways. Sometimes the viewpoint of the designer needs to flex – a young Black person might design a very different community campaign to an older White woman.

Often working in public services and sometimes in charities too, community research (work that could easily create the scope of the work or identify solutions) is often met with alarm.

Just like the teacher in the school, people worry. What if they ask for something we can't do? Better not to ask, then people can't complain. What if they find out we haven't got the power or money to change what really needs to change? We can't just give people a blank page!

The frame to dance within helps in these situations. If we define the boundaries and background of the work, then the page is no longer blank. We can ask the design question that begins the dance between reality and possibility. The Healing-Centred Design framework provides us with the frame we need for trauma-informed, supportive change. By creating energy, connection, inspiration and possibility we jump over barriers caused by insecurity, apathy or adverse experiences and everyone is able to do brilliant things.

Within these boundaries, and with this understanding… what might we create?

Dance with Healing-Centred Design

When I described the 'frame to dance within', did you light up? Often people living with pain, trauma and injustice crave security, regulation and solidity. We need both, the certain and the uncertain, the solid and the dream-like, and the frame to dance within gives us both: safe walls and open space, boundaries and opportunities for imagination.

Let's move this framework off the page and embody its structure to feel its power. Imagine a diamond shape, the bottom pointy end represent pain and the top pointy end represents power. Hold your hands out in front of you, touch thumbs and index fingers together forming a diamond space between your hands. The pain you want to change is between your thumbs, the power you can create is focused at your fingertips. Allow your other fingers to meet, resting together and keeping the diamond shape between your hands. Within this space you hold all the practices, principles and processes you need to concentrate and focus your power. Imagine power flowing through the diamond and out of your fingertips, creating the ripples of change you and the world needs.

Embodying the pain to power transition means it is always with you. When you see or feel pain, touch your thumbs together, recognize it's there then allow your fingers to meet, breathe in the sense of focus and strength this simple hand gesture creates. Draw on the principles, processes and practices you have developed in reading this, and within your own healing work, and that you are constantly adding to and evolving.

Back to your paper, draw a big diamond and let's practise using it.

1. At the bottom pointy end, identify a pain that you want to address. Choose something simple and note it down in a few words.
2. Then imagine what an empowered version of this would look like. In a few words write this at the top of the diamond; this is the change you want to create.
3. Next spend some time thinking and making notes in the space between the top and the bottom, in the body of the diamond.
4. Identify the principle that would be most useful in creating this change (rhythm and ritual, filter, collide and align, transition, contribute and benefit). What resonates?
5. Add a process you will use to create movement between the two points (a recipe, some instructions, a method).
6. Note down a practice that will support you along the way (think holistic, creative, sensory, behaviour-based).

Finally, draw an arrow pointing upwards next to your diamond. This simple framework with your content can guide your intentions, and plan and frame your communications, reminding you and others of a goal, shifting your perspective and setting out your change journey.

Here's a quick example:

- **Power** (that you want to create): Representation in leadership.
- **Practice**: Listening spaces to sustain activism and prevent burnout.
- **Principle**: Individuals should have equal opportunities, rights and treatment.

- **Process**: Story gathering research to identify opportunity blockers.
- **Pain** (that you want to change): Discrimination at work.

The brief

Now it's time to refine your ideas about what you want to create, solve or heal. It's time to create a brief. Let's recap on the journey so far.

In doorway one, we explored the pain you want to change. Did you identify a personal challenge, a social problem, a societal inequality? Maybe you want to create change that will improve your life or improve your family's wellbeing. Maybe the change you dream of will impact everyone.

Doorway two introduced the principles that can move you from pain, personal or societal, to power – collective, embodied power. The kind of transformative power that makes anything possible.

In doorway three, we are designing processes and strategies, creating the pathways that change can channel through.

A brief is a short document or set of instructions that provides key information and guidelines about a project, task or issue. It is used in lots of sectors including design, business, law, marketing and media to ensure everyone involved understands the objectives and expectations. Sometimes it might be called a 'Project Initiation Form' or a 'Kick-Off Sheet' but I first experienced using and working to a brief in art collage. A creative brief is less about formal structure and more of a frame to dance within, the creative constraints inspiring creativity. The resources you have available can shape your brief. Limitations can become activators for your most powerful work. The collage artist, Henri Matisse, who worked with vivid colour, contrast, paper cut outs, paint and dynamic compositions said, 'Much of the beauty that arises in art comes from the struggle an artist wages with his limited medium.' In this nugget of wisdom he is describing how limitations can be catalysts for creativity, encouraging us to explore new possibilities within defined boundaries.

Remember the Dream Collage you designed at the end of doorway two? Pull out your Dream Collage or notes from that activity. Let's reflect on these questions again and write ourselves a brief.

Do you know what raw ingredients you have?

People, environments, materials and wisdom can all be resources to add into the recipe for change. Raw ingredients ready to be blended, mixed and transformed. Maybe you have personal ingredients to add in: courage, experiences, love. What wider ingredients could you draw on? Is there a relationship with a business that could be fruitful? Have you left someone hanging who said, 'If there is anything I can do to help, let me know'? Can you recycle or repurpose what you have?

What kind of transformation do you want to make?

How do you want the transformation to feel? Who will see and experience it? What does your Dream Collage and collected notes tell you about transformation?

Then you can add the frame, the parameters.

Consider the things that are more defined or fixed in your work to change things. It might be the time, money, people involved or place you are working. They might not always stay fixed, but it's helpful to set out this frame. I like to draw a box and label each side to remind me of the parameters. Keep it simple by choosing just four to start with. Common parameters for design work are:

- Budget/resources available.
- Time availability/timescale/urgency.
- Cultural, seasonal, environmental or political considerations.
- Materials available.
- Reporting or evaluation needed (usually for client or funded work).

Creating the Dream Collage

I often describe the change process like an ice cream machine. The moving parts, the elements, all have a function and must work together to achieve the outcome. Handles, cogs and levers create momentum, tubes and tubs contain ingredients, paddles mix and churn, energy freezes and moves ingredients through the machine. To create those flavours of change, those nourishing, supportive, connection-focused outcomes, the raw ingredients need to be transformed. Something needs to happen to change milk, fruit and sugar into delight.

In our Dream Collage, the moving parts might be people, communications, education or skills. Momentum might come from pressure, desire or fear. The energy might come from money, kindness, ideas or increasing need. The handle might be an organization, a platform, an event. Some of these parts are strategic, parts designed to work together with other parts to create a greater whole. Others are cultural, a set of behaviours, agreements and ways of being that contribute to the bigger picture.

Putting it all together

Using these headings and have a go at writing yourself a brief.

1. **Raw Ingredients**
   - People involved
   - Environmental context
   - Materials and equipment
   - Personal ingredients
   - Wider resources
   - Things you can reuse and repurpose

2. **Vision for Transformation**
   - Desired change
   - Feel of the change
   - Audience
   - Inspiration

3. **Frame**
   - Budget
   - Timeframe
   - Contextual considerations
   - Materials
   - Reporting

4. **Components**
   - Moving parts

- Momentum
- Energy
- Key structures

Lighthouse learning

When I'm working with more structural things, briefs and a frame, I regularly need to go back to my imagination to keep me feeling inspired. But I know returning to my watery daydreams I can get lost in the imagination part of designing, so creating a balance between these two parts of me is important. Flights of thought whisk me off to naïve shores of idealism and greater good. Sometimes I'm pulled down with a thump if I don't stay aware of my grounding in reality. Healing-Centred Design blends the wild imagination with the grounded knowing and widest perspective with step-by-step progression. To be healing-centred is to be attuned and committed to learning and reflection, both needs that infuse daydreams with solidity and realism, and depending on what and how you learn, can keep a good dash of awe in the mix. How formal education has developed over the years is an interesting example of how context and environment can change our learning needs.

Learning Mass Education began in the UK in 1902 (to give you a reference, that's ten years before the *Titanic* sank). This was a radical change. Previously, there had only been a few government-funded schools and other voluntary schools run by religious organizations. Most children's education was done in the drawing rooms of the privileged, on the farm or the shop floor of the factory. Massive inequalities existed in both the access to learning and the quality of the learning, most often connected to class, economic status and social circumstances. The ambition of this change was to create a more equitable learning experience for children.

The mass education school was a place to learn. Schools held knowledge artifacts: books, educational tools and writing equipment. They also had teachers who were knowledge sources and providers. These artifacts and teachers were only accessible within schools, and schools were only accessible to some. Mass education meant that access was widened to these learning materials.

But there was and is a problem. How these learning materials were used, and are still used, is not accessible to all. Just creating a provision does not mean that everyone can access it. If you are ill, disabled, think differently, or are poor, in pain, traumatized or have additional responsibilities, access to learning will be compromised. In fact, if you need to learn in a different way, if you are interested in different things, if you have particular skills or strengths, unique circumstances, interests or personality, have physical or emotional requirements or transport needs your access to learning could be compromised. These descriptors include many of us. I bet you read one you identified with.

When schools are set up as the only standard place to learn, diminishing access and diminishing quality go hand in hand. If I cannot get into the classroom, I cannot learn. But schools are not the only place we learn. They are just the only state-endorsed place children are required to learn in, with standard curriculum that educates the masses – sometimes.

But learning artifacts, providers and tools are not just found in schools. Information has exploded with the internet. You can learn anything, any time in nearly any way with a touch of a button. With Artificial Intelligence you do not even need to learn. A machine learns and produces faster than we can comprehend; we might not even need to prompt it with a question. Algorithms mean machines can create and produce what we need before we have even thought of it.

In this new age of learning, education is on a *Titanic* course, a sinking ship. Why are we teaching children to memorize by rote when that skill is not needed? Why are we teaching the same history we taught 50 years ago rather than educating on the daily shifts in politics, the environment and conflicts that will affect their future? Bias, privilege, irresponsible leadership and lack of knowledge, failure of machinery and structural issues alongside the iceberg, have all been blamed for the *Titanic's* failure to sail its course. Probably the disaster happened though a combination of all these issues. Systems of education display these elements too.

So, can we imagine something different? Beginning with you, what could your lifelong learning experience be? Can you change how, when and why you learn?

If you are not following mass education, if learning opportunities are everywhere, and there is a vast sea of knowledge and experience you can sink into, swim through or float on, how will you be guided?

The symbol of a lighthouse has been showing up for me recently. A dream, a picture on a friend's wall, a model made from a paper tube and pom poms by a colleague's child, in words and images in my work. I've always been drawn to coastlines, particularly the faded glamour of seaside towns' piers, chipped pastel railings and old ice cream signs. The boundary between land and sea scattered with shale and shells, the odd chip fork and sea glass glinting. I can see myself walking empty shorelines, gathering and looking out to sea, my back to the land. Or sheltering from the wind, sitting on a checked blanket, hugging my knees and leaning on the bleachers as the clouds swirl above the water. I can hear seagulls and distant fairground noises, sweet candyfloss mixing with salty air tang.

When I place a lighthouse in the scene, it rises from the shoreline, solid and reassuring. The bold red and white stripes are striking against the greyish mist of the sky and sea. It sits on rocks slick with seaweed and blue mussels. A doorway humanizes the sculptural form. I think about how much care and attention it must take to keep the painted walls so pristine, such a clear beacon visible far out to sea. I think about its purpose, guiding sailors in to land, helping ships navigate their course and avoid the blackish rocks. The lighthouse keeper might never meet the sailors they help, never know the stories of the ships, yet they show up, polish the lamp, repaint the stripes, keep a look out to sea, rest and live in the place where they can make a difference, knowing that these repeated actions, executed with skill, keep people safe again and again.

A lighthouse and its keeper has purpose, and every part of that structure contributes. Form follows function. The height, shape, size, position, colour, internal and external space, patterns of the keeper's tasks and behaviours, are all shaped to enable humans to help humans, avoid disaster and enable safety.

The lighthouse can guide our learning too. These questions, inspired by the purpose and structure of the lighthouse, and the life of its keeper, can create a new type of curriculum, one focused on learning with purpose, safety and direction:

- What lights you up?
- What can your light illuminate?
- What can you see around you? What can you see on the horizon?
- Where do you notice change?
- Where can you rest, eat, live? How can these spaces support your purpose?
- What do you need?
- What do you need to develop skills in?
- How do you care, tend, repaint, clean, polish and create patterns?

Systems mapping

If we see the lighthouse, then let's make a map to help us navigate. Systems thinking and systems mapping are ways to visualize the whole picture rather than just one part. Phrases like 'the bigger picture', 'everything is connected' and 'domino effect' nod to this way of thinking and it's used to describe interrelated processes or address complex problem-solving in many sectors. Examples showing the approaches' adaptability include Finland's education system, which uses systems thinking to create holistic curriculums that link subjects, encouraging critical thinking and innovation, and Greta Thunberg's Movement, which links environmental crisis to economic policies, consumer habits and political systems. You're as likely to find systems thinking approaches within

NASA, Tesla, IKEA and Google as well as within campaigns like Black Lives Matter and the United Nations that uses systems thinking in its Sustainable Development Goals (SDGs). Systems thinking is a concept worth knowing about.

Thinking in systems helps us understanding how different parts of a situation, organization or community (or all three of these!) are connected and interact with each other. Instead of focusing on individual parts in isolation, systems thinking encourages us to look at the relationships, patterns and feedback loops between them. Systems mapping is recording these patterns in ways that show us how they are joined up.

For example, in 2019 The Food Systems Map was created by the Rockefeller Foundation and highlighted systemic issues like food insecurity, inequity and climate impact globally to help organizations, policymakers and innovators to reimagine food systems for 2050. As useful as it is globally, systems approaches are useful on a personal level too. As we have explored, chronic pain is influenced by biological, psychological, social and environmental factors. Systems thinking and mapping applied to chronic pain can help us see connections and recognize that solving one problem might involve understanding and addressing several different root causes or symptoms.

Teaching systems thinking

'Let's make a joyberg!' A sea of blank faces stared back at me. Most faces had a lanyard hanging beneath and a few wore uniforms. This gathering of workers, frontline practitioners, clinical staff, people who organized services and decision makers, were sat in a grand town hall room that was stiff with history. I stood in front of a decorated fireplace with my paper and brightly coloured oil pastels and could feel prickles of curiosity, apathy and judgement.

Above the faces I could see thoughts buzzing around the room, unsaid conversations happening. My joyberg announcement didn't help settle the room! Why are we here? I don't know! I was told to come. Isn't it something to do with the funding? Who is she? I've not seen her before. Where is her lanyard? This room is stuffy. Am I supposed to be here? Oh god, she's got crayons. Oh no, this isn't teambuilding, is it? Where is the coffee? When can I leave!

We were all there as part of ongoing work to connect people across systems and organizations to improve how families are supported. Everyone was connected by the shared goal but did not yet see the threads of connection and experience that were woven between them. Our work together over six months would weave this group and many others including parents, children, young people, grandparents, services, systems, communities and businesses to create a rich tapestry that we were calling a community of practice.

I had been planning to use this session to explore systems thinking as a way of problem-solving and looking at the connected whole rather than individual parts.

I'd been driving to the session, thinking about activities like this that we could use, and my plan was to find some shared problems and challenges that are faced across the system, then use systems thinking to address some of these challenges. I noticed I was feeling a bit flat, unusually for me on my way to a workshop as I'm usually excited and energized by these meetings. Following my feelings and inner nudges is a practice I am, well, practising, so I followed the thread and realized it was the focus on system-wide problems that was making me feel demotivated. What if... my inner voice said... we looked at joy instead?

I didn't have enough time to plan and rethink the activity in detail, but I was familiar enough with systems thinking that I thought I could pull it off! I had my bright oil pastels in my bag from a different session and thought I could use the bright colours to bring some brightness into the room.

I knew as soon as I asked the check-in question that the idea would work. 'What brings you joy?' Answers were unexpectedly deep, the room relaxed as people found overlaps and connections, faces lit up when we used systems thinking and conversation to explore the topic more, with prompts to see the multidimensions of the topic. What patterns bring joy? Who is involved? Where does this joy happen? What are we assuming? What are we valuing? How could we create the conditions for joy?

We used a classic systems thinking 'iceberg' exercise, one I've often used as a diagnostic to identify where in the system the challenge sits – above or below the surface. But this time we created joybergs, colourful drawn out models with rainbows of layers, visualizing the joy we see and feel and the patterns, processes and beliefs that contribute to its creation. The exercise wasn't about diagnosing, it was about creation. How might we create more joy in our lives? As we were in a work context, motivation at work came up and possible changes were explored in working patterns, ways of changing routines and priorities, ways to collaborate across organizations and share resources.

I've used joybergs multiple times since. It's become one of our core activities and I'm always surprised and delighted in the depths people feel able to go with this activity, and how the energy shifts when we focus on joy. Often, people who have experienced this activity bring it up with me months later. Joy exploration is memorable and the systems learning and following action that comes from using this as a topic is valuable.

Make a joyberg

Want to have a go? Grab some brightly coloured pens and use a blue one to draw a wavy horizonal line across the page, about one-third down the page; this is the sea line. Then draw out a wobbly diamond filling the paper to represent an iceberg. You want a section above the sea line and a larger section below the sea line. Using different colours, split the under-the-sea line section into three horizontal sections. Label the top section above the sea line 'visible', the section just below the waterline 'patterns', the section underneath that with 'structures' and the bottom section 'values'. You can find a template for this exercise on our website www.brilliantthing.co.uk/make

- **Visible:** In the top section, free write for five minutes about what you can see in your life that brings you joy. You can use the space inside and outside of the iceberg above the sea line.

- **Patterns:** Review your writing. What patterns do you notice? This could be patterns of behaviour or repeated themes. What comes up more than once in your writing about joy?

Write down your thoughts in and around this section called 'patterns'.

- **Structures**: Think about those patterns. What creates them? Who or what is involved in those patterns? What systems or activities could you put in place to create more of the positive patterns? How could that work?

  For example, If you want to create more joyful time with friends and notice a pattern of desire for this bubbling up in the mornings, could a regular early morning walk work for you both?

  Write down your thoughts in and around this section called 'structures'.

- **Values**: Our values, beliefs and assumptions play a big part in the choices we make. When thinking about options you have identified, what values, beliefs and assumptions help you move towards joy?

  Write down your thoughts in and around this section called 'values'.

- **Reflect**: Step back and look at your iceberg as a whole. You have visualized a whole system around creating joy with your thoughts and words. What stands out? Are there any actions you want to take? What do you want to reflect on more? How do you feel?

Design thinking

Design thinking means thinking like a designer, but there is a whole industry and theory that sits behind this framework.

Systems thinking and design thinking have much in common – both place humans and connection at their centre. Systems thinking gives us lots of insight about the context and complexities, and design thinking is used to create specific solutions to complex challenges. Both approaches are best friends when used in 'co-production'.

Co-production means that the people who are going to benefit from the thing are involved in producing it. In community work, co-production has gained momentum and is often seen as the gold standard for community engagement and service design. Co-production is rooted in collaboration and shared responsibility: a range of people work together as equal partners to design, deliver and evaluate services, initiatives or solutions. For example, a new, co-produced school might be developed by a group of people including children, young people, parents, teachers, community members and future employers. As well as designing the school, this group would also contribute to the delivery of the lessons, cooking of the lunches, organizing of the day. Within the co-production group, time would need to be spent understanding and aligning the differing needs, desires, experiences and ideas within the group. You can understand why co-production needs time and support! Often co-production can feel like going round in circles and additional pressures begin to influence the work such as internal conflicts and how people feel about lack of progression, time and money constraints. I have seen a brilliant co-production project implode with these additional pressures that are generated by the process itself. I have used design thinking, in combination with systems approaches, to avoid this problem and to guide personal and societal change work. Let's explore what design thinking is, and where else this methodology is used.

Where did it come from?

Design thinking isn't a new concept. The phrase was coined in 1969 by economist and Nobel prize winner Herbert Simon, who discussed using design as a science for thinking. More recently Tim Brown of IDEO popularized a five-phase design thinking model: Empathize, Define, Ideate, Prototype and Test. The British Design Council articulated the Double Diamond model, adding in Design Principles and Method Bank to the core model to guide and shape the work.

What is it?

All these frameworks begin with a challenge, end with a solution and follow a similar process to guide thinking through a number of exploratory stages. There is a rhythm to the process of opening up perspectives before refining ideas, developing, expanding and trying out different versions then using the testing insight to develop a tailored solution.

Expand, contract, ebb and flow. It's a rhythm that aligns with Healing-Centred Design and provides a container that allows movement through the process change, with some certainty of direction and progression. We like to use the British Design Council model in our work and name the phases: Discover, Define, Develop, Deliver.

Where is design thinking used?

Design thinking has been used in start-up phases by companies like Airbnb and Uber, in the development of global health initiatives and tech companies and in communities to create positive change. Initiatives such as the Voices for Birth Justice Campaign harnessed the power of empathy and creativity in addressing pressing issues and unlocking new opportunities using the framework.

In practice

To bring the methodology to life in personal and societal change work, here are two examples. One is about creating a personal change, the other is about creating a societal change, both using a design thinking approach to develop a solution.

Project 1: Personal change: Improving sleep with chronic pain

Discover
- Talk to people with back pain to learn about their sleep problems.
- Find out what makes their pain better or worse.
- Learn about things that might help with back pain and sleep.

Define
- Figure out what part of the problem matters most.
- Decide what we want to achieve, like sleeping better and feeling less pain.
- Create a design challenge question.

Develop
- Think of different ways to answer the design challenge question. Think in imaginative, radical, global, local, big picture, detail – generate lots of ideas.
- Try out some ideas with a small group of people with back pain, learn what works, look for surprises and patterns.

Deliver
- Make the best ideas better based on what people say.
- Make guides to help people use the ideas, and connections to build community support.

Project 2: Societal change: Reducing chronic pain costs in the UK

Discover
- Find out how much back pain costs the UK; consider people missing work, spend on painkillers and accessing support.
- Ask people who experience the pain, bosses, doctors and leaders what they think about these costs.
- See if other places or industries have good ideas to help people live and work with pain.

Define
- Figure out what would make a big impact. Addressing root causes? Producing cheaper help? Everyone having more money?
- Decide what we want to do; use a design challenge question to frame this.

Develop
- Explore ways to answer the design challenge question; take inspiration from nature, children, industry, history, technology. Find ideas everywhere.
- Try these ideas in different places with different people and see what the impact is on costs and people.

Deliver
- Make the best ideas real and easy for everyone to use.
- Work with leaders and groups to make sure the ideas keep helping people and saving money.

The 'design challenge' question

The design challenge question is an important point in the design thinking framework. It is the lever that is crafted during discover/define phases and creates momentum and parameters within the develop/deliver phase. We like to spend time getting the wording of this question right and follow this basic structure:

- **How might we...** (opens up with curiosity)
- **Change...** (defines specific problem)
- **Using...** (identifies our ingredients)
- **To...** (shared intended outcome)

The design challenge question cannot be created at the start of the process as we have not gathered enough insight or worked out what matters yet. Posing the question too early could lead to us going off track or creating a solution to a problem that does not exist! The question can pivot a project. Notice how these two similar questions could lead to very different solutions:

- How might we change how people experience chronic pain, using friendship and kindness, to enable people to have fewer sick days at work?
- How might we change how our company operates using our line management processes, to enable people to take time off without impacting overall productivity?

You can see from these examples, skills in research, communication and collaboration are beneficial and there are overlaps with co-production, particularly in the develop phase. An array of tools, from empathy grids to journey mapping, are available online and I'd encourage you to use your personal interests and strengths to make the process fun and engaging. Groups who participate in these sometimes playful, creative learning experiences find connection and trust and feel empowered around creating the change. An ethos of co-production, layered with a framework of design thinking and a whole system approach, can create the frame you need to dance within.

Collective action

Collective action means multiple people creating momentum through their individual actions. It's the experience of everyone pulling in a unified direction, in their own way. Collective action doesn't mean everyone doing the same thing or following the crowd. Within collective action, each person has agency and control and has chosen to move in a direction that aligns with others around them. Collective action creates momentum together that would be impossible to do alone.

Pain can often feel solitary; a singular experience felt by just one. The power that a healing-centred, resilient and brilliant approach brings moves us from solitary to solidarity. People standing together taking action, creating change.

Spaces of belonging

To know how to take collective action we need to have a shared understanding of our purpose. Everyone needs to know something about each other, even if that is the just that we swim in the same seas. Finding these threads of connection can be tricky in a world where brands are all things to all people, algorithms tailor their stance and position based on who they are targeting even when the product is not tailored to the individual, and politicians seem to flip flop towards or against options depending on who is listening to maximize votes.

When we invite people into places and pay attention to creating a sense of belonging, even if those people have a different opinion or experience, we can create valuable work. Sometimes this may look like an open mic night, a cosy coffee shop, a reflective practice circle or an annual event. Maybe it's a shared circumstance or cause. It could also mean a platform or online group, or even a group of colleagues gathering around a shared project.

Creating gatherings and spaces of belonging provides opportunity for people to find those connections in between, discovering hidden commonalities and overlaps that spark solidarity.

Clay on the wheel

We have to get clay on the wheel before we make the art. If we are going to create change, make something new happen, shift or transform something, we need to start with the raw ingredients: ourselves, our ideas and our experience. This is the clay we are working with. If you don't know how to create collective action towards change, start with you. Why do you care? What matters to you? What are your needs, tender parts, healing opportunities? Self-development, organizational development and societal development all need you, and so the more you understand about yourself and how to support yourself, the more possible all these things become.

What does it mean to get clay on the wheel? Well, you have to start somewhere. If you are going to shape a beautiful vase or a joyfully wonky plate, it starts with getting the raw material and the tools. So you have to put yourself out there somehow. In words, written or conversation, in pictures or videos, you can ask questions, apply for jobs, share music, dance, perform poems. You can make banners, compile research, send emails, keep a journal. Showing up can happen in so many ways, but there has to be some element of visibility, even if that is just getting things out of your head and onto a page, working up to sharing that page with others. People who nurture their raw materials have brilliant ideas. Ideas are magnetic – if you put them out there in the world, they attract in people.

Wide stance, soft focus

If 100 people wrote 10 letters each to a local authority leader lobbying to stop a community centre closing, they might be able to influence this decision. If 100 people, wrote 10 letters each to different local authority leaders expressing personal experience of the social, economic and health benefits of the community centre, this would create potential for politicians with different agendas to see why the community centre was important, potentially even becoming advocates themselves. While neither option gives a guaranteed approach, going wide and keeping the message pliable can create greater influence and more collective action.

Make it memorable

The best collective action is memorable. This is why I love creative examples of people making change together. Artist Candy Chang transformed a neglected space into a vibrant community where people could have meaningful conversations about death. Now 'Before I Die' is a global project, and there are 5,000 message walls where people leave messages of hope, aspirations and reflections on death and dying – powerful work. Collective action that is memorable and inspiring provides stories for people to tell and pass on, sparking other people to take the idea and run with it, creating a ripple effect of change.

Your turn

Craft a 'How might we' question using the structure below then feed it into an AI tool and ask it to generate 20 answers to give you some new ideas for collective action:

- **How might we…** (open up with curiosity)
- **Change…** (define a specific problem)
- **Using…** (identify ingredients that we bring to the table)
- **To…** (create collective action)

My example:

How might we create a memorable opportunity for belonging, using creativity and storytelling to create inclusive and collective action?

My AI generated ideas:

1. Story quilt making
2. Collaborative street art
3. Holistic healing circles
4. Memory walking tours
5. Reviving abandoned spaces as community hubs
6. Midnight feasts to raise funds for a cause
7. DIY workshops
8. Mobile inspiration libraries
9. Flash mobs
10. DIY recycling initiatives
11. Skateboarding events reclaiming public spaces
12. Free bike repair sessions for community mobility
13. Experimental cooking classes with foraged food
14. Architecture projects about creating accessible spaces
15. Poetry challenging norms
16. Anonymous postcard project
17. Fashion shows promoting body positivity
18. Street games for older people
19. Urban wilding
20. Renewable energy art installations

Organizing

There are many ways of organizing and structuring collective action around change. When you have generated some interesting ideas, you might like to think about how to organize to make them happen. In America, the term 'community organizing' traces back to the early 20th century when grassroots movements sought to empower marginalized groups to address systemic inequalities and improve their living conditions. Barak Obama began his career in community organizing and this shaped his leadership philosophy. In the UK, community development started to become embedded in local government and non-profit strategies in the 1990s. National Lottery funding, which started in 1994, strengthened community development work in charities and voluntary groups. Austerity and the Conservative government's 'Big Society' agenda aimed to improve community resilience but did not lever in enough resources and the pandemic reinforced the importance of community development, leading to the 'Levelling Up' agenda. These political agendas and social shifts rely on organized community development and collective action. Here are some formal and alternative structures for organizing and gathering for change:

- **Charity**: Charities are official groups that help people by collecting money or goods, like clothes or food, and they give them to those in need, usually without expecting anything in return.
- **Social Enterprise**: Social enterprises are businesses that want to make a difference in the world while also making money. They sell products or services, but instead of just focusing on money, they care about helping people or the planet too. Profits are reinvested in the community.
- **Cooperative**: Cooperatives are groups where everyone works together and makes decisions together.

They can be about buying things, like a grocery store, or working together, like a cleaning company where all the workers own the business.
- **Community Group**: Community groups are just regular people who come together to do something good for their neighbourhood or town. They might clean up a park, organize events or help out people who need it.
- **Inclusive Communications Teams**: Dedicated representative groups focused on ensuring that communication strategies and materials are accessible, inclusive and culturally sensitive to all members of the community.
- **Action Learning Sets**: Small, peer-led groups that meet regularly to tackle real-life challenges, learn from each other's experiences and take action to address issues collectively.
- **Reflective Practice Forums**: Structured gatherings where community members engage in reflective discussions, share insights and learn from their experiences to improve individual and collective practices.
- **Critical Friends Networks**: Supportive groups where members provide constructive feedback, challenge assumptions and offer alternative perspectives to help individuals and organizations critically reflect on their work and decisions.
- **Murmurations**: Small gatherings of five to seven people who are part of a bigger collective movement. These smaller groups come together in informal ways, to build connection, contributing to the momentum of the bigger movement; inspired by the collective

movement of birds in flight. People might be part of multiple murmurations within a larger group.
- **Thematic Networks**: Groups or communities organized around specific themes, topics or areas of interest. These networks bring together people with a common interest or focus, and work best when they hold a budget, resource or responsibility that they can use to make change.
- **Convening Gatherings**: Active gatherings that bring people together to discuss, collaborate or take action on a particular topic or issue. They provide facilitated opportunities for networking, knowledge exchange and matching asks and offers.
- **Parties**: Social gatherings or events organized for the purpose of celebration, entertainment or fun. They are opportunities for community building, relationship building and bonding.
- **Community Soups**: Democratic events where community members collectively decide how to allocate a portion of public funds or resources empowering citizens to prioritize and fund local projects. Often food (soup) is served to all costing a small amount of money. The fee from the soup sales is added to the funding pot.
- **Citizen Assemblies**: Representative bodies randomly selected from the community to deliberate on specific issues, providing input and recommendations to inform decision-making processes.
- **Campaign Group**: People who share a common goal or belief and work together to bring about change using various tactics such as advocacy, lobbying,

protests or media campaigns to raise awareness, mobilize support and influence decision makers to enact policy changes or societal reforms.
- **Action Group**: Groups of people who focus on proactive measures such as community organizing, grassroots activism or hands-on projects to address problems, create positive change and empower local communities.
- **Listening Groups**: Organized and supported gatherings where individuals facing similar challenges or experiences come together to provide mutual encouragement, understanding and assistance. These groups offer a safe and supportive environment for participants to share their thoughts.
- **Public Living Rooms**: A free, relaxed space for people to sit, get together, chat and share a cuppa without an agenda. They can foster belonging and connection and were popularized by the UK organization Camerados who encourage people to 'look out for each other'.
- **Book Club**: A gathering focused on championing a cause or promoting a type of author, for example, an environmental book club or Black writers book club. These spaces pool knowledge and build awareness.
- **Exchange Event**: A tool exchange, clothes swap, skills swap or bring and buy sale is a community initiative that provides a free or low cost place for people to access the things they need, without having to purchase them outright.
- **Summits and Camps**: On or offline events for learning exchange, inspiration, ideas and connection,

often focused on a theme, topic or issue and can engage large numbers of people.

◡ Threshold: What do you want to change?

The power Healing-Centred Design creates transforms experiences in personal, team, organizational, community and societal development work. We get to choose how and where we channel our energy. We also get to experiment and change our minds about what we want to change and how we want to use our energy and attention.

All big challenges have individual and societal, personal and collective elements. Each of these can be supported and amplified by some well-designed processes. Sometimes we just need to start with one corner to turn the page. So, what do you want to transform?

What do you want to change?

Pain	Power
Individual chronic emotional + physical pain	**Personal** empowerment, leadership + purpose
Societal injustice, inequality, marginalization + oppression	**Collective** community action, social movement + systemic change

Case study: Maff Potts, founder of Camerados

Maff Potts, founder of Camerados, is a social change pioneer with a rich history of creating culture change in homelessness nationally. He led the UK Government's £170m programme to modernize homeless centres and ran the largest homeless services for The Salvation Army. Maff inspires connection and kindness, combating loneliness and creating community by drawing on his own lived experience and creating a platform for others.

> Do big shifts happen in the light or the dark? This was the question that lingered after meeting with Maff Potts. He created 'Public Living Rooms' through setting up Camerados. These rooms are informal spaces made for connection, set up in unexpected places, like outside on the street, in prisons, inside domes or in public buildings such as libraries.
>
> I have known of Maff since I worked in the NHS, when we brought one of Camerados' domes into the hospital. It was an igloo-like structure that housed a Public Living Room. The Public Living Room space had sofas inside and signs that encouraged staff and patients to just 'be alongside each other' and share stories. People behaved differently in a cushion and fairy-light filled space, dotted

with yellow mugs, postcards and pin badges. It was a radical act to put such a homely and inviting space inside a hospital, with minimal rules and an open invitation.

After arguing with health and safety and selling the concept to many other departments and directors, we got the dome installed and I personally witnessed beautiful, tender moments of people being human together inside it. Slightly at odds with Camerados' ethos of unprogrammed spaces, a gorgeous pet therapy charity called Noah's Ark filled the space with white bunnies on launch day! It definitely felt different to shabby waiting rooms or a sterile lobby.

During that time Maff gave a talk to the people helping to share the message of the tent and Camerados. I remember he was struggling with a health condition and needed some adjustments to give the talk. Despite being in obvious pain while sharing his story, he was also very aware of not centring himself in the Camerados movement. Instead, he highlighted the brilliant people who had got involved. I remember wondering about this and wanted to see and hear more of what was driving this powerful movement.

When we met again six years later, I asked Maff about this and he told me about a formative experience, volunteering in a homeless shelter after losing both of his parents at a young age. The isolation and grief he felt after their deaths compelled him to spend his first Christmas volunteering at a shelter. He expected to give support but discovered something much more transformative. The people he met, people with far less resources and living in really hard situations, helped him through his grief in ways he hadn't anticipated. This shift in perspective redefined how he saw charity, community, social justice and his role in the world.

Maff shared that for a long time he went to the dark places to create transformation, often working with people that did not want or recognize the power of perspective change. This seeking of the places where there is most resistance, as places where he must work, was reinforced as Maff often walked to work thinking, 'I hate this – I must be doing the right thing.'

We wondered if this was because Maff had been in a dark and painful place of grief when he had that formative enlightening and powerful shift of perspective, and so he might have subconsciously recreated that situation in his early career because he knew the shift was so important.

Now, the social movement he has co-created, Camerados, is a place to find light in the dark. But don't be fooled by the cushions into thinking this has happened by chance. Look carefully and you might notice an elegant set of processes, practices and ways of organizing and reconditioning occurring. These include principles like 'Ask someone who is struggling to help you', an ethos of accepting people as they are, organizing and disrupting hierarchies by encouraging people to take charge as needed, and a way of organic scaling by engaging those who are genuinely interested in the ethos. Deep attention is paid to the visual, sensory and emotional experience of their 'Public Living Rooms'. People love being part of them and there are now over 250 Public Living Rooms in six countries.

Maff and Camerados provided me with some formative experiences that have influenced how I see the world. I experienced the sharing of grief between a woman who had just lost her husband and didn't want to leave the hospital and go home as she felt like she was leaving him, and a man recently released from prison who did not have a home to go to so had come to the hospital. As I had been sitting in the dome reading on my lunchbreak, they had struck up a tender conversation and

I listened quietly, holding my breath at the beauty of the moment of connection and being seen that they were experiencing.

But the learning was not just about what was happening in the dome – it was the ridicule and disinterest I faced when presenting the idea to the hospital directors. It was in the anger of the security team at no one being in charge. It was the cleaner who didn't know if she was allowed in the space and was afraid she would be seen as slacking off work if she read the stories written on postcards in the space. It was the pressure from the charities working locally to use the dome to run sessions, and the boundaries that were needed to be held to keep the space unstructured. It was also in the surge of gleeful power that I felt when we landed the dome and the mix of ego and activist parts of me behind this feeling. It was the way the visual prompts – a blackboard, mug and badge – helped the Public Living Rooms and people who got involved to feel part of something bigger.

Look carefully and you can see the threads of this influence through Healing-Centred Design.

Maff recognizes his privilege – a White middle class man – and sees his role as getting out of the way and making himself smaller. The

> sentiment behind this stance is a beautiful one but left me feeling a bit sad. I wish I'd challenged him on that and suggested that maybe it's about creating space to let everyone get bigger, turning the dial up on everyone's shine so we can all benefit, and that includes letting the world see his own, un-dimmed light.
>
> https://camerados.org/

◯ Reflective practice: Ideate it

What is it?

A symbol-seek is a creative way to engage with your surroundings and generate ideas. By stepping outside with an open mind, you can discover visual connections to the reflective questions that shape your journey. This activity invites you to notice patterns, symbols and stories represented all around you.

How do I do it?

Choose a location that feels inspiring, whether it's a park, your neighbourhood, a city street or even an indoor space. Choose a question or topic to reflect on, maybe reflecting on your personal development or something that is blocking you. Begin walking slowly and intentionally, letting your surroundings guide you. Look for details that catch your attention – shadows, textures, contrasts – and allow them to speak to the questions and topics you're considering. You might like to take photos, collect pebbles or leaves, pick up leaflets, draw the details or jot down some notes.

What next?

When you return, look at your photos or objects, drawing or notes. What have you discovered? How can your insights support you? Choose one or more of the objects to represent this journey. This object becomes a symbol and joins your growing collection of treasures. Use symbol-seek often to spark new connections and insights, allowing it to inspire your ongoing journey of transformation.

4

Doorway four: Practice

Doorway four leads to a courtyard, an expansive walled garden with shady trees and meandering plants. The sun is shining and a cool breeze dances across the grasses. This place is peaceful and warm, wild dog roses scent the air.

Here is where we practise. We try out our processes, spend time healing, feel through the change we are creating. We will journey outside of these walls to a cliff edge and return to celebrate with a feast. The weather will change and we will adapt, creating layers of support and understanding around our change work. Notice how you step into this doorway. What are you bringing with you? What do you leave behind? What will you find here?

Fizz: A poem for finding

I went there.
We met there.
Walking towards the edge with easy steps and settling, like we always knew we would, on the mossy cliff edge.
The world tumbled on, out of sight beyond the rolling hills, protecting our pocket of quiet.

Here I am, you said.
I am here, I said.
Our words, a beat out of step, landed together on 'I'.
You can read me, so I see my thoughts reflected.
I can feel you, so watch a galaxy of connections spark.
The words tumble out, ideas on top of ideas, angles shift, mirrored.

Reflecting, sparking.
Practising exploring.
What if and when, how and why, back and forward and in between.
Blending and touching, escaping and draw back in.
Except we are not the only ones here.
The quiet settles and we watch the salty fizz and weathered rocks.

Broken, unbroken.
Could that be us?
The question floats away and melts into the horizon.
Sharing a breath, I'm not sure who asked it.
Maybe we have always been here, sun warm on our backs, mossy grass and sea glass.
Out there, there are rock pools to explore, a whole world of people and places to discover.

Free to find, safe to leave,
When the quiet comes we can come back here
Here to re-find.
I plucked a daisy and picked off three petals.
The horizon smiled.

By Kerry Tottingham

Healing-centred practice

You have created this garden in your mind, this safe space. Take a moment to look around and drink it all in. Safety lets us make mistakes. This garden is beautifully imperfect, comfortable. Here we can practise. The word 'practice' refers to the repeated application or exercise of a skill, activity or belief with the intention of improvement or making something happen. We describe practice as the combination of feeling, thinking, doing and being, blended to create momentum and movement towards change.

Healing-centred practice involves effort and commitment designed around your core needs and biggest hopes and aspirations. The practices I choose are about empowering, supporting, creating and evolving. Practice can be personal, like my artmaking practice, or systemic like the rhythms we create in organizations around workflows and time we spend together and apart. If process creates the structure and form, practice creates the layers and motion. Practice can be cultural, setting norms, expectations and influencing how people act and behave. A project I know of has a success measure that is reached when someone says something like, 'It's just how we do things round here'. A brilliant example of a practice becoming rooted in a place.

Reflective practice is our go-to practice at A Brilliant Thing CIC, which flows through everything and supports what we do, and it's an approach that softens how I move through my life with chronic pain too. Reflective practice is a process of continual learning, changing position from being in the work, to stepping outside of the work and looking in. I love to add a creative element to reflections, using materials to express, process and unravel often mixed feelings and complex experiences that unfold during the change work that I do externally and the personal development and healing I work through internally. Conversation-based relational reflecting is beautiful too, in couples or groups, and helps build a strong sense of collective power.

Here are 20 healing-centred practices that might be useful in social change, organizational or personal development work that you do:

1. Reflective practice
2. Free-flow word association
3. Journaling practice
4. Creating workflows
5. Wobble rooms
6. Conflict resolution
7. Empathy groups
8. Active listening circles
9. Walking meetings and street wisdom explorations
10. Community engagement events
11. Boundary sharing
12. Creative campaigning activities (banners, performances, installations)
13. Restoration and upcycling work
14. Affirmations
15. Breathing exercises
16. Horizon scanning
17. Play breaks for grown-ups
18. Grounding meditations
19. Gratitude list making
20. Mentoring experiments (try reverse, group or speed mentoring)

Feeling

Healing has to include emotion. Paradoxically, when we have experienced pain or injustice, we have a tendency to numb or dampen our emotions to avoid the feeling of pain. Through this journey we have been building up practice and processes, ways of being and doing, recognizing and supporting our needs and awakening our imagination. You may have noticed prompts in these pages, asking how you feel, but it's time to focus attention, time to attune with our emotions. So what are you feeling?

I used to hate the question, 'Where do you feel it in your body?' Asked by well-meaning bright-eyed women's circle members. At the time all I could think (there's a clue!) was, 'In my head! Not in my body! It's all in my head!' In those patchouli soaked circles, I watched in delight, fear and curiosity as my wise woman friends, people I rarely saw outside of circles but spent intimate hours with in this monthly ritual, expressed their feelings. One night it was stormy and hot; a summer storm had been building and the energy was intense. Feelings in words had been shared but we all felt an oppressive energy, something more to be released. We moved as one outside, started stamping and dancing, willing the rain. I had never expressed my feelings through my body, but in the dark, in this group, with these women channelling emotion, I danced hard and felt big. We stamped and clapped and raindrops started to fall euphorically.

It's taken me a long time to recognize that those bodily pockets of discomfort, pleasure and pain do not need to be immediately zipped up into my brain, interpreted and reframed as a neat package of thought. Instead, feelings can be complex and shifting and live within you.

When feelings are oppressed in society, they intensify. My dad recently had an operation. They left a small, open wound so any infection could leave the body rather than trapping it inside. I think societal wounds are like this too. Without the space, time and safety for emotional release, emotion intensifies, infectious and powerful. We see the boiling up of emotion in riots, violence, outward explosions or in apathy, defeat, accepting of the unacceptable, overwhelmed by the pain. Both options cause extensive damage.

Getting lost in emotion, the opposite of repressing emotion or restricting feelings, can be a reaction both of pain and pleasure. Grief can create a feeling of emotional overload, a seasickness of feeling, and what comes after can be a shutdown; numbness as we try to cope with all the feelings. In marginalized communities, repeated questioning from authorities about how people feel and the following expression of feelings without action, leads to research fatigue, tokenism and breakdown of relationships.

Feeling your way through is like using a sixth sense, an emotional sense – intuitive. In our Healing-Centred Design model, feeling is what happens when we connect pain and practice. Practice means intentionally developing skills, knowledge, capacity and meaning through repeated actions and efforts. We might have a yoga, arts or mindfulness practice, or we might engage in a sports or academic discipline, or a wellbeing regime. Sometimes we can describe a collective of habits as a practice. With the understanding that to change pain we will need to engage in a supportive practice, we can use feeling to identify and motivate us.

When we expand 'feeling' to include emotional understanding, moods and trends, sensations, influences and perceptions, we recognize the active nature of feelings. We can follow the inspiration, empathy and feeling of connection that arises when we view pain through an emotional, feeling lens. Feeling can help us intuitively find practices that work for our needs, desires, preferences and circumstances.

When addressing pain in our bodies, feeling will provide valuable information on how we are experiencing. For instance, the stretching in a movement class or the impact of a medication. Connecting with our emotions while pausing in the green of nature will share insight into how we can regulate. For example, the feelings we identify in a busy street, an art gallery, on a train or in a hospital help us understand how environments affect us. When addressing societal pain, recognizing the feelings, mood and perceptions of the group and the different people within the group can provide needed understanding of the potential actions, reactions and possibilities to explore.

Supported spaces where people can express emotion, with reassurance about what will happen next and commitment to transparency about how this emotionally charged information will be used, is vital. There is a lot to consider here. Cultural and experiential knowledge and understanding might restrict what is shared and with whom. External factors or personal identification might shape where and how feelings are shared. There might not yet be a common language or understanding of feelings. Expression of feelings can help heal bodies and communities. Create a practice of nurturing, feeling-filled relationships with yourself and others. Build trust, cultivate openness, offer and protect time and space to listen and you can lead transformation.

Leadership

How do you feel about leadership? You might see society valuing leaders with advantages that few possess. You might see these advantages causing harm, self-perpetuating, showing up as white supremacy, classism or ability bias. Many leaders we see around us lie and cheat and don't care. The idea of being a leader, in its traditional hierarchical and power wielding form, for many, has lost its shine.

Revolution leaders

But there is another type of leader, a leader who organizes for change, tackles inequality and fights for others' lives. Consider Kathleen Wrasama, an Ethiopian-born British community organizer who came to England in 1917. Facing personal trauma she turned this into action, leading an organization dedicated to improving communities and the lives of Black people in the UK.

Or 'The Quartet', four women – Elizabeth Anscombe, Philippa Foot, Mary Midgley and Iris Murdoch – who shaped philosophical thinking in the 20th century, and revolutionized how we think about ethics, courage and justice.

Or Joseph Galliano, who steadily built the charity Queer Britain from nothing to open the UK's first LGBTQ+ museum with a mission to preserve histories that have been ignored or destroyed.

Or Northern Power Women's Person with Purpose 2023 award winner, Alison Madgin, who set up Samantha's Legacy to educate the next generation on the dangers of knife crime, inspiring with 'Knife Angel', a structure made up of 100,000 surrendered knives.

Undercover leaders

Many uncelebrated and unknown leaders are also working on the ground to change systems, educate, hold to account and build new realities. I'll tell you about some I know. The person I know who spends hours every week teaching older people to connect through simple tech tools. The quiet attention of the admin worker coordinating supplies at the foodbank every week. The mother who encouraged her son's school to celebrate International Women's Day. The community mediator researching previous experiences so she can be mindful of her language choices in a new group. The person who turns up with a smile and energy to every session. The person who shows up even when they are feeling low. The person who shows up after slipping up.

Here is another idea about leadership. Mutual aid describes the phenomenon of spontaneous, informally-organized groups, community coming together in hyperlocal areas, often using WhatsApp or social media platforms, and using their skills or time to help each other. Taking action at the grassroots, leading responses together. Remember the pandemic street WhatsApp shopping groups, local prescription delivery by the biker group, neighbours checking in on each other? The swaps, doorsteps dinners and childcare bubbles?

Many more people had a taste of the fulfilment that comes with offering and receiving support without the expectation of paying for a service or guilt for relying on people without being able to give back. Charities, institutions and local governments reacted to these new ways of helping. Some embraced the extension of support, were inspired to remove barriers to people helping each other and used their resources and access to Personal Protective Equipment (PPE), like masks and gloves, to support these groups. Others attempted to formalize, constitute and wrap in red tape.

- **Mutuality**: Both nostalgic and radical – still feels huge and different.
- **Leadership**: Spontaneous and compassionate – now feels different and possible.

Thinking

Feeling is important for healing and so is thinking. Conscious, mindful thought followed by action is powerful. So taking time to explore what and how you think builds your own power and capacity, but thinking alone does have its limitations. My coach, Beth Creedon, uses a concept called 'strong suit' to identify the amour you wear to keep you safe and protect you. Thinking is my strong suit. She explained the flipside of any armour, including thinking, is that it's heavy, uncomfortable, awkward and limiting.

When faced with a challenge, experiencing pain or uncertain about my next move, my go-to response is to think my way through. It's served me well. I have delved into learning concepts and methodologies, read research papers to increase my understanding and perspectives, listened to podcasts about thinking. I have fallen asleep to recordings of Alan Watts, the British philosopher who popularized eastern philosophies in the west in the 1960s. I have woken up to the rousing messages from the 'Small and Mighty!' podcast series from the United Nations Trust Fund to End Violence against Women.

Thinking alone can be lonely. Have you ever been so in your head that you have forgotten about your body? Forgotten your core needs for food and rest? Caught up in thinking as a coping mechanism for avoiding pain? The extreme end being dissociation to the milder experience of forgetting to eat causing dysregulation in your body, which over time could cause health and wellbeing challenges.

Being in your head is a learned coping mechanism. Living in thinking, without feeling, doing or being can impact your mind, body, work and relationships. Thinking, feeling, doing and being are interconnected aspects of human experience that shape our existence and influence our actions and perceptions. Having an awareness of the need to spend time in each experience, each day, and understand how they connect and interplay for you can have a profound impact on your life.

If we are looking to heal pain in our bodies, then we need to think and learn about treatments, reflect on what is right for us, plan when and how to try options and evaluate their effectiveness. If we are looking to heal pain in society, thinking can help us understand the problems from different perspectives. We need to seek examples of what has worked elsewhere, plan and coordinate experiments and interventions, and choose and review approaches.

Identity

Let's think about identity. Communities of identity can mean people connected by geography, commonality in personal traits or shared experiences. We can find identity in a community or as inhabitants of a place. We can be a member of a society or belong to a club. These groupings and structures hold power to change individual experiences into collective happenings. In social change work, particularly if local authorities, corporates or big institutions are involved, people are grouped and described as residents, tenants, clients, customers, service users, the public or citizens. These identifiers can hold an innate power imbalance and centre the difference between people. Sometimes in community work, to equalize power dynamics, more inclusive terms are used like humans, folks, or simply, people.

Citizen

A citizen is a person who has rights and responsibilities in a place or situation. Citizenship describes a legal status and an identity.

'Citizenship' can be a problematic term due to its exclusivity, reinforcing systemic inequalities and historical ties to nationalism. Citizen meaning legal status often marginalizes undocumented immigrants and perpetuates imbalances based on factors like race and class creating an oppressive power structure. The borders and edges that the term creates can limit ideas of solidarity and expansive community. Often rights and responsibilities are tangled into identity, particularly when identity is framed by citizenship.

Participant

A participant is a person who is actively involved in a place or situation. Participatory action describes engaging, contributing and taking part, expressing, shaping and affirming an identity or vision.

'Participation' offers an alternative power structure inclusivity, empowering marginalized groups and challenging traditional power structures. It involves active engagement in and promotes collective decision making and collaboration.

In transformation work, when referring to a group, I think it's helpful to use a term that describes an active identity, a word that describes what people are doing rather than who they are in relation to others. I have settled on the language of participant, participatory and participation as it can be used to describe both individual and collective identity and activity. I like the Latin roots, the combination of 'pars', meaning 'part' or 'share', and 'cipare' indicating 'to take'. The recipient is passive, the participant is active. Share and take, give and receive. This balance of contribution and benefit is vital for social change and found in our fifth principle.

Doing

I've got an action oriented identity. I like action and I know I need reflection to balance that out. Are you always doing? Do you know someone like that? Inaction is not my comfort zone. In the feverish first days when I got covid, I wrote two blog posts, knitted a scarf and bought multiple books. During my recent recovery period after an operation, as soon as I had a little energy, I cleaned the house top to bottom, stalling my recovery and giving myself a ton of pain in the process, before I let myself rest properly. Writing a to-do list for a week gets me hyped up and I try to do it all in a day. I have told stories that mix up laziness and rest, and regularly shush my inner critic as she cackles that 'advice to stop is for other people!'

Action taking can be a power that develops in the messiness of lived experience. Learning to take action to move through chaos or start things before you know how they will end, because starting is better than stopping, is an experience many who have experienced trauma will recognize. Action taking can be a form of avoidance and disassociation or be a superpower that propels you. What's happening around the action taking, the context, matters. Let's explore how action – doing – integrates with thinking and feeling.

Does your action taking most often revolve around work, your relationships, a chosen role, a hobby? I notice I explain what I do in relation to where I spend my time and sometimes mix up 'what do you do', with 'what do you care about'. Thinking and feeling happen internally; the expression of feeling is the vital channelling, the movement between internal and external worlds. Doing is the action, the tangible steps, behaviours and efforts in the responses we make that demonstrate our thoughts, feelings or ideas. The birthplace of action can be thought or emotion, or both. Doing from a place of thought, reflection, knowledge and discernment can create change, but without the emotional understanding and perceptive lens that comes with feeling, our actions can be hollow or damaging.

Some example of action that comes from a good place, but might become damaging, that I have experienced include:

- A hospital decision maker focused on fast service success measures, who prioritized patients with easily fixed issues, creating record treatment time data.

- A community centre manager who feels so deeply for the families who use her supportive groups that she opens the doors around the clock, but then needed to close the doors for three months while she recovered from burnout.

Actions and visibility

I once worked with someone who only went by her first name. She was equally brief about her life, never revealing anything about herself. In work she identified as an activist but her projects were solo and rarely discussed, covered with a cloak of invisibility. I presumed the activist work happened elsewhere and had the distinct impression that she thought I was too young or too stupid to share the action with. I found this closed door to communication unsettling. I felt her presence but couldn't see who she was. I felt her distrust keenly and responded with the same wariness. As someone who is careful of the people I surround myself with I wanted to build a picture of her and struggled with the rigid boundary she held tight. The things she did do or say publicly formed a sparse cartoon-like impression of who she was in my mind, and I can't actually remember her face. A story that sticks with me is the rare insight into her life, an argument with the postman on the doorstep because she wouldn't give a surname. Looking back with empathy, there might be a hundred and one reasons why she pulled a blackout blind around her life. Maybe even for the same fear rooted reason that I like to know who the people are around me. This lack of openness made her actions invisible too.

This memory comes up when I think about action because I think action and visibility are linked. While I love the idea of Random Acts of Kindness (small, spontaneous, often unseen actions that help spread kindness), I also love the idea of visible kindness. Seeing people pick up litter deters people from dropping it. Kindness can be contagious.

Sometimes doing feels impossible, preventing movement or overwhelming us. Doing can also have a particular flavour of judgement attached. 'You should be doing…' or 'You are wasting your time…' or the favourite, 'Just get up and do it!' But healing steeped in doing isn't the same as reacting, pushing through or performing. Doing infused with intention and purpose is more like catalysing, nudging, sparking and inspiring. We can ask our body questions and listen to its suggestions for what to do:

- What could I do to redirect my pain?
- What does my pain need?
- How can I nudge towards ease or pleasure?

Doing might be seen in big actions, such as policy change and demonstrations, and in the small actions, such as finding a new perspective, posting photos to highlight a problem or asking for help. Visible, spontaneous action weaves with multi-year programmes to change systems; action happens on the front line and in the authority offices, in communities and in schools, in political spaces and public places. When we can't see each other's actions, blame seeps in: 'They are not doing enough!' 'When did they do anything for me!'

Perhaps the most important action we can take is to make healing visible in the way we do things. Sharing information to remove friction between services, setting up platforms so people have space to speak and listen, building relationships so they can call on each other in a crisis or celebration, pooling resources so everyone gets access to what they need. Purposefully redefining what is yours, mine and shared, taking action towards a bigger picture. Thinking shapes what we do. Feeling makes what we do matter. Doing it with purpose and intention creates transformation.

Nourishing

The best solutions are nourishing and lasting; they mend and tend. Solutions take time and experimentation, attention and care, an understanding of impact and consequences, intended or not. Sometimes a quick fix might be right, other times it's lasting solutions we need. Which is better for healing?

Healing can be a quick fix. Your body quickly seals up a papercut, heals a scuffed knee, repairs a broken bone. But if that bone broke because of abuse, the fix won't stop the problem. When the broken bone is healed alongside relationships, power imbalances, confidence, care and support, maybe the problem can be solved.

Post-traumatic growth sees healing as recovering from the physical, emotional, psychological or spiritual wounds caused by a traumatic event or experience. The recovery from these wounds also involves the positive change that can come from the experience of overcoming hard things and healing and might look like personal strength, relationships, spirituality and new possibilities or perspectives on life. Though post-traumatic growth focuses on the healing journey of the individual, I believe communities and organizations can experience this same recovery and growth.

In 2019, I started a job in a lead role for a charity who provided infrastructure and support for the community sector. This involved developing a team to deliver training and support around legal structures, funding and volunteering, and working with the local authority and other partners to make the experience of living and working in the place better. The team was to be set up in a place that had not had infrastructure support before, and which was different to the areas that the charity already operated in. New place, new team, new job – and I was working without a blueprint.

We started with conversations. Many, many conversations with organizations, volunteers, project teams and people that lived there. We soon realized that the place was fragmented. There was competition between charities made worse by the way funding was organized. There was no map of the system, creating information privilege, reputation and rumour-informed relationships and favoured organizations had built empires that included some and excluded others. I didn't use the word healing at the time, but reflecting on the three years I worked there, healing is what we were doing. Healing relationships, processes and systems. Healing to improve the flow of resources and money, creating spaces for mutuality and support and providing learning experiences in ways that encouraged information equity. Over time, collaboration and partnerships strengthened, organizations started working together on shared outcomes and the relationships between people changed. Healing was still in progress and while the threat of external forces, political change, crisis in economics, health and care were near, the sector was far more resilient after consistent support to heal. This was evidenced in the profile of the sector, the income flowing into the place and in how forums had transformed into networks. Transactional partnerships had become spaces for co-creation, people were more welcoming and had more tolerance for change. This type of transformation is dimensional rather than sequential. It's a feast rather than a recipe. Sometimes we need a recipe, in the same way that sometimes we need a fix, and sometimes we need multiple things bubbling at the same time – a feast.

A recipe

A tart blackberry, steeped in sugar, warmed with heat, stirred, cooled and jarred becomes jam sweetly spread on your bread. The blackberry is sequentially transformed from tart to sweet, from a hedgerow treat to a bramble jelly brightening your morning.

A feast

As the blackberry jam bubbles in the pie, hot from the oven, sweet steam mingles with fragment rice, vivid vegetables glisten with melted butter and ladles accompany full dishes of tempting sauces and crisp pastries. I think of that scene in *Hook*, a film I loved as a child that reimagines J.M. Barrie's *Peter Pan* and tells the tale of a band of pirates on the fictional island of Neverland. The pirate boys are known as 'lost boys' because they fell out of their prams and were not claimed within seven days, meaning they were sent far away to Neverland. In the film, the abandoned lost boys imagined up a delicious abundance of food, joyfully scooping up tasty treats that no one else could see. Their glee and happiness at conjuring the food, eating together, deliciousness tumbling onto plates contrasts with the lonely abandonment that had brought them together in the first place and filled up my emotional memory too. With this multidimensional experience – imagination, food, play, magic, sensory, emotion – the lost boys discover joy and power to change their experience.

Dimensional transformation is change that happens across multiple layers of experience in individuals, communities and organizations. Dimensional transformation is full, rich and multifaceted and leads to significant changes in perception, understanding, behaviour and structural systems.

Being

If you are going to create change, play a part, catalyse, reimagine, who are you going to be? Will you be a mosaic of your experiences, a collection of parts, gathered together in a human shape? Will you be an expression of your history or a declaration of the future?

Is being your state or your stance a condition or an approach? As time passes, will you be different or the same, changed or unwavering? Will you leave an impression or a trace of scent in the air? Is being momentary or rooted?

When I left a job, which I felt like I had made my mark on, I asked for feedback from partners, friends and colleagues; a review of what they had valued about our work together. I was writing a diary, which I later turned into an email series about navigating change and transition between job roles. I was on the lookout for patterns and trends, hoping to bring this insight into my next role. One word came up again and again – calm. Calm handling of difficult situations, helping others feel calm, calm under pressure. Though I was flattered, it didn't quite ring true. As I reflected on my time in that role, I could see how outward calm had been useful, but I knew that often internally it had been quite different. Not chaotic, but definitely with a vein of panic and fear pulsing underneath. I cope with these emotions with a need to control and focus, and slightly detach. It was this I think that was interpreted as calm.

My body certainly wasn't calm. It was during these stressful years that the pain started to engulf me. On the surface I was steady, but my body had started screaming. The more I stayed in control, the more my body rebelled. In response to pain in our body's being is the connection and relationship between thoughts, wisdom, feelings, emotion, surroundings and internal and external environments. Being calm feels like a place I am discovering. Calm is warm, comforting with a cool breeze. Calm is sitting in the basin of a shallow valley, near water, green… blue… quiet. Calm is when the inside of my experience touches the outside of my environment with an imperceptible porous boundary between the two. I'm not trying to get out of my head or into my body, protect from the outside or escape into the surroundings. I am embodied.

'Be the change you wish to see in the world!' A spiritual slogan splashed across Instagram and birthday cards. What about 'being in change'? Being in change, in progress, in the middle of things doesn't feel very calm. In flux, it feels messy, tangled, unfinished. But we can't create change without working through the ambiguous. Let's be the change in all its messy glory and make it hyper visible as we go.

Being can be dream-like. We dream with no conscious effort at night and drift off into imagination by day. Dreaming is a natural state we practise in childhood, using our imagination, creating scenarios, exploring concepts and wondering through what ifs.

Dreaming of an equal, just, supportive society feels like a radical act and a complicated equation. What are the choices and trade-offs? How can we get the right answer? Our conditioning dismisses exploration of these questions and calls our dreams naïve. But what if our starry dreams led to the resources, support, energy and power to bring those soft-focus dreams into precise definition?

Navigating

There are still bright realms and misty spheres to navigate. Dreaming is personal, creative and can happen in moments. A flash of colour or scent on the breeze can awaken a desire. Making intentional choices to follow the path, make the art or create the memory, is the act of turning the dream into a reality. We can shape the outcome by the small choices we make en route. Sometimes we forget this. We can get swept up like children in misty moments, following stars that don't align with our values or succumbing to instant gratification without responsibility. Then, rather than shaping the dream, the dream is shaping us.

A sense of powerlessness can seep in when we follow dreams that are not our own. We validate, excuse and try to align, and before we know it that's just the way things are. We are conditioned to let others' dreams shape us. Consider who benefits from the insta-gratification of an impulse buy following a pop-up promise. And yet, there is that gnawing knowing that something else is possible – our own dreams. In an unfair world, some people have the privilege of choice, taking action on the things they desire. Others have to fight through discrimination and clamber over barriers and thrash paths through tangled bias. But for each of us, an inner star flashes when we intentionally make choices that align with the change we want to create.

Tending

We've spent time together, delving into who you are, how you are in relation to your body, your community, your world, finding places to mend and tend. We have spent time thinking about why you do what you do, why you want to make different things happen and who that might impact. Let's tend to your soft strengths.

Changing your personal world or changing the world we live in requires strength. But this isn't the moment you need to armour up for battle. This is where we need to discover the soft strengths within you. Imagine an egg, its precious inners protected by a shell that is strong enough to provide a safe home for the growing bird, yet vulnerable enough that the baby bird can peck its way through when ready to emerge. The shell may hold against the jaws of a fox for a time, but the nest and maybe the parent, added layers of strength, keep the egg away from harm. Soft strength is the shell, the nest and the caregiver.

The term 'strengths based approaches' first came into my awareness when I started to do more community organizing work. The phrase was coined in the 1990s and has its roots in psychology and social work. Charles Rapp wrote *The Strengths Model*, which focused on 'amplifying the well part of the patient'. The popularity of his approach spread quickly, and in 1999, Dr Martin Seligman, the president of the American Psychological Association at the time, made an observation that fuelled strength based practice:

> The most important thing we learned was that psychology was half-baked. We've baked the part about mental illness, about repair damage. The other side's unbaked, the side of strength, the side of what we're good at.

In community organizing, this approach meant identifying the strengths within a community and the strengths of people that live, work and play in that community and drawing on these strengths to organize and take action on community priorities. So if there was a vandalized playground and people wanted to change that, a non-strengths based approach might be to pay for an external company to come and fix up the park. A strengths based approach might explore:

- Could we draw on the strength of the relationships between parents outside the school gates to spread an important message?

- Could we use the local library to hold a workshop to explore different ideas?
- Could the youth group help us design the new park?
- Could we ask businesses in the neighbourhood to run donation schemes?

Strengths based approaches can take longer. There is a need for in-depth engagement in communities, adapting and revising of plans based on learning about skills, capabilities and ideas that exist already in the place. It takes listening and understanding of aspirations and shared desires. There can be conflict too, differing strengths to align. But the pay-off for using strengths based approaches can be huge.

A community garden I worked on was in the centre of an estate in Greater Manchester. The estate had some amazing people living there, resourceful, committed and kind, but people there often expressed that they felt forgotten and undervalued. Over the years, one by one, places where people could gather had been closed down. Youth centres, community centres, pubs and shops, once adding vibrancy and community spirit had closed their doors. Underfunded and under-resourced, the area had social and environmental problems. But the community spirit hadn't died. The local organization I worked for was invested in the place and had been established there for 20 years, creating and supporting, doing projects and holding festivals and celebrations. The community garden was a long-forgotten project in a public space that used to be looked after by the youth centre before it closed down. There were raised beds and accessible gravelled walkways, but litter and weeds were rampant.

We didn't have a lot of money, but we began with some helpers, clearing the area. As it was so visible, dog walkers and people passing on their way to the parade of shops would shout out to us: 'Good luck with that!! It'll be ruined in a week!!' It appeared there wasn't much hope but soon the area was clear. A local gardening firm helped us plant donated plants, and some of the dog walkers offered us a hand too. It was a hot summer and the ground was parched, so a neighbour let us run a hosepipe from their house each morning, watering the thirsty new fruit trees and herbs. Another popped by with a full watering can when he could in the evenings. The youth service ran a drop-in football session on a Thursday evening at the kick pitch near the garden so the teenagers could see people working and the progression – we always worked later on a Thursday. The teenagers didn't join in, but we often got hellos and cheeky questions. The banter felt like a way to connect and we welcomed it with laughs and smiles. A school group came down and planted the planters, cheery colours and shapes, and the shop goers started stopping for a chat, telling us about their gardens. Soon it was ready, just in time for the community festival that weekend. But then we got a phone call from our watering can neighbour early on the Friday morning – the fruit trees had been stolen!

Like wildfire, WhatsApp groups started pinging and when we got to the garden, people were crowded round. A few months earlier I think we would have heard 'I told you so!', but the conversations were different – people were talking about how to fix this together. Within the day new plants were bought and donated. People who had never helped with the garden before were digging and restoring the garden. The school had promised that their nature club would tend to the garden and youth workers and the library had started thinking about a joint funding bid for an outdoor skills project.

On festival day the small but beautiful garden was perfect, and even though some weeds have woven themselves in between the flowers, and sometimes the plants need a bit more care, each year one or another organization, community group or bunch of neighbours take it upon themselves to run a project or have a get together to tidy things up before the festival. This low level tending and community ownership works. The garden isn't perfect, but it is cared for. The soft strength in this community tending feels very different from the 'fighting vandalism' approach, with posters about fly tipping and uniformed patrols used on other parts of the estate to try to clean up areas.

So what does this mean for us? What soft strengths can you find within yourself and how could you centre your change work around these strengths? My soft strengths live in my creativity. I have learned tough influencing skills. I can plan, negotiate, organize and demand action. I can bring out my hard strength to fight and protect, but the most change I have created has been using softer, tender strength. I feel this strength in my body; there is a still awareness, a widening of vision and perspective. I can gently allow creative thoughts and actions to bubble up, and guide me to make choices, choose words and write down ideas. My soft strength comes with seeing more deeply, listening to my intuition to understand more about why something is happening and what is needed.

For years and years I wanted to write. I wanted to write my story, I wanted to write novels, document my research, write down my ideas, thoughts and learning. I wanted to write to inspire and be inspired and to make up poems and touch people. I yearned to write, but I did not write – I was afraid. Writing seemed too dangerous. I was afraid of my own imagination, my own creativity. I was afraid that once I wrote things down they would take on a life of their own and run away. I wanted to keep my words and ideas close. When I did write, in formulaic ways, funding evaluations, job applications, reports, I loved the boxed-in freedom to express, but often wrote long explorations in those boxes, exceeding word counts that I then deleted.

I bought journals and diaries and courses to help me write, then filed them away. One day, at a time in my life when everything felt boxed in, my yearning was extreme. Lists I decided, I will just write list after list after list and keep them in one big book. Lists of shopping, jobs, recipes, housework. To-dos and jobs done, lists of camping gear and freezer meals. My lists started mundane but slowly opened up a bit. Lists of dreams, life themes, my strengths, what I wanted. I started using sentences then rambling paragraphs. My lists jumped onto my laptop, the big book with pages full of lists and thoughts started giving me ideas for stories, imaginings. I started writing disconnected jumbles of fantasy and memory and manifestos. The ideas didn't really make sense and the thread of story was tangled, but the words were spilling out at last.

I had used my hard strength (organizing, planning lists) to find my soft strength (musing, creativity and intuition). At a time when the walls around my life were thick and immovable, I felt a freedom and joy escaping into the writing, somehow free of the judgement and fear that had kept my words inside me for years. And then I couldn't stop! I kept writing and exploring and imagining and playing with my creative strength. My business was created. I was able to engage in therapy for the first time. My words were used in campaigns and events and this book emerged in a way that tended, repaired and expanded me and my world, growing the garden of change around me.

Layering

I hope you are buzzing with ideas like bees in rose bushes. I hope you can feel the beginnings of change in your bones as the sunlit garden awakens and warms you. I hope you can see how the energy of pain can transform into powerful action to make things better.

And maybe, you are conscious of feeling overstimulated? When I am overstimulated my senses are electric. Noise and smell are my biggest warning signals and I can feel physically punched in the face with either. In an overwhelmed state I feel like general chatter is a cacophony of sound shouting in my ear. Too much all at once, at full volume, can reduce me to a puddle on the floor.

I heard the most beautiful expression of the experience of neurodiversity from an unexpected place. While sitting with my hair turning a sunset shade of pink, my hairdresser told me about her daughter asking about the daily pills she takes. She explained to her:

> I am so creative. I see the world so brightly and in technicolour. It feels like I can see everything all of

> the time through all of my senses. These tablets mean that when I am here with you now, I can focus just on you.

I thought this explanation, the shift it created, was powerful. Rather than saying everything was so overwhelming and she needed pills to block things out, she explained things differently. And it was exactly her neurodiversity that let her think about this in this way.

As someone with chronic pain and sensory issues, things can become overwhelming very quickly. I am usually coping with a high level of background pain alongside running a business and tending to a busy, blended family. So adding more into that mix can make my patience pot bubble over. Usually that looks like a shutdown for me, or a wave of bigger pain. For others this might look like an explosion, a burnout or a fire. Often pacing is advised for chronic pain; this is about managing your energy and expectations, reducing activity and upping rest. While I agree theoretically with this approach, I struggle to follow it. What works for me is layering.

Layering starts with you and then builds out into the work you do then the change you make in the world. Imagine geological layers; horizontal layers of rock or soil that have distinct characteristics, textures and colours. These layers provide insights into the Earth's history, with each layer representing a different period of time or geological event. In a similar way, you can create layers to support you to move through pain and into powerful change.

Layer 1: Essentials

Begin with your core and essential needs, the bedrock to your support. What needs must be met while you are living with your particular flavour of pain (physical, emotional, environmental, structural, social, organizational)? There are the basics (water, food, shelter) and there are essentials. For me, being near water, a bath, pool or a hot water bottle is essential to manage my pain. Time alone to process, often walking or creating sketchbook pages, is an essential. If I go too long without these processing spaces I lose my sense of who I am underneath the pain. I call these needs essentials rather than basic as the word basic, to me, suggests simplicity, minimum or a lack of complexity, which I find easy to disregard. Essentials are things I pay thoughtful attention to.

Layer 2: Comfort and joy

In primary school I remember singing a Christmas carol that included the phrase 'comfort and joy'. Years later I had a pink poster with this phrase in bold red letters hanging on my university wall. But it took me until my 40s to really take this phrase to heart and I feel I am just at the beginnings of learning and feeling its power. You might expect comfort and joy to come later in the layers, a sprinkling on top of all the more serious layers of support maybe. But comfort and joy enriches the soil, creates goodness that other habits and practices can root in. Microdosing comfort and joy might include soft blankets, candles, a dog stretch, noticing the sunlight on a freshly wiped surface, an aroma, a bowl of deliciousness, a song, the burst of spring or flakes of snow.

Notice, allow, practise being open and aware, and comfort and joy will pour in and fill micro moments, like sand filling gaps around rocks of pain.

Layer 3: Faith

I don't mean religion here, though you may have structure around your faith. I mean what do you believe in? What are your core understandings? What do you stand by? What would you fight for? I believe everyone can create brilliant things in the world. I believe some people have less access to the things they need to make those brilliant things, and I believe that is wrong. I will fight for justice, equity and change so that people can create without discrimination or pain or unfair circumstances limiting the brilliant things inside of them.

Layer 4: Spaciousness

Practise this by curating your bedside table. Our bedside tables hold the things we need before sleeping, in the dark of night and that we want first thing in the morning. It's often the first thing you see holding our go-to stuff. We all have our 'go-tos'; these are the people, places, things or ideas that we reach for when times are tough. I challenge you to curate your bedside table to include objects that represent your go-tos or help you move towards them. I challenge you to remove the clutter.

My bedside table holds a book, a manifesting journal (bought for me by my teenager even though he is very cynical about these things!), my pain medication and some sweet-smelling relaxation oils. All these items add layers of support to my day and move me towards the change I want to create in the world. But my table also includes bottles of vitamins I don't take, a chipped cup and some scrunched up receipts. As I look at these, the vitamins are berating me for not taking them, the chipped cup doesn't care about me and the paper debris reminds me of the housework I must make time for. These are not supportive of the focused, calm, person I am cultivating and so they will go. Extend this thinking to your wider surroundings. What is limiting, creating barriers, distracting or extracting? What is enriching, improving, fertilizing?

Layer 5: Enrichment

Surfacing beyond our own needs, enrichment, beliefs and surroundings are what we layer on the topsoil. Topsoil contains the highest concentration of organic matter and nutrients because it is formed over time through the weathering of rocks and composting of organic matter. Your topsoil layer is formed through the experiences you have had and learning you have gathered, composting together to form a nutritious layer that supports you and enables growth. This top layer of support is not about creating a barrier between your pain and the world, it's about everything your pain has taught you, enabled you to see and feel – how your pain has pointed to the changes needed and demanded it is heard.

This topsoil needs nurturing – it's vulnerable to the elements. To keep it healthy, don't dig it up too much and try not to squash it down. Change what you plant in it every now and then to keep it strong and add nutrition. Avoid toxicity seeping in and water with care. Allow the sunlight to warm the earth and let the layers of support you have created nurture you.

◡ Threshold: Where and when to transform?

When things are broken and when people are hurt, we need Healing-Centred Design to transform things. When you see or feel pain in people, places, nature, systems, communities or environments, mending and tending are your pair of tools for change.

Where and when to transform

Individual + Societal Pain

↓

Mend + Tend

↓

Personal and Collective Power
(Brilliant Things)

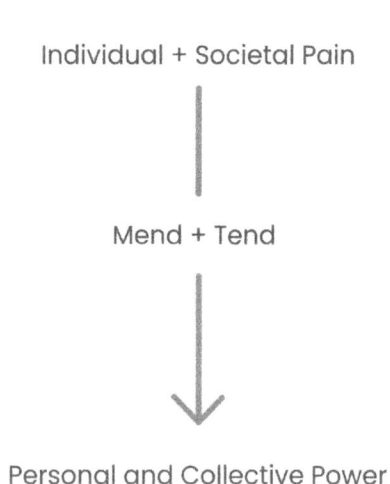

Case study: Tamu Thomas, founder of Live Three Sixty

Tamu Thomas, founder of Live Three Sixty, former social worker and author of *Women Who Work Too Much: Break Free from Toxic Productivity and Find Your Joy* is a leadership coach specializing in supporting over-functioning, high-achieving women. Her personal journey through anxiety and low mood led her to establish her wellness brand.

> Why do you want to talk to me? Tamu levelled a warm but direct look at me, inviting me to share while communicating that this conversation needed a purpose. With that look and the unfolding conversation, I felt the years Tamu had spent in places that looked purposeful but felt painful.
>
> Why did I want to talk to Tamu? Her social worker background intrigued me. Tamu is well known and respected as a somatic coach and author, but despite her glossy website and beaming social media, Tamu doesn't come from the typical 'corporate burnout rebranded' story – she has grit. When I explain this difference she disagrees. Social work is corporate, she assures me, corporate without the cash. The bad bits of governance, policy, budgets, AGMs, spending cuts and savings

all described like the cutthroat business of corporate life. And social work is traumatic. Dealing with the chaos of generational trauma, struggling to make a difference and fighting against rules and decisions that play with people's lives. From the outside looking in, Tamu explained, social work is about caring, looking after people and social justice. But on the inside, it can feel hopeless, battling a broken system with people's lives at stake.

Tamu was not born to suffer, so the choice to go into social work seems offkey, but Tamu has hope inside her. An unwavering, certain trust in humans' capacity, ability and strength. She went into this work because she believed in her own ability to make a difference and believed in strengths based work to meet the needs of people. Tamu told me about families she helped, foster children her mum looked after and care settings that worked. For Tamu, healing means regeneration, spirituality, activism, deep care and justice. But within the confines of the social work corporation, a place where Tamu had to fight for people, where access to resources was scarce, where she was being let down often, this hope was being crushed.

Tamu has experienced 'power over': coercive control, dominance, gatekeeping and decisions that inflicted harm. But making a difference doesn't need to break your heart. 'Power with', she reflects, was found in her best social work: partnerships with other agencies, sharing information, collaboration. Power infused the wrap-around care and careful support that people needed, but it was a richer, softer power, a power within and between us, a power we hold. Power, she describes as alchemy.

Where does Tamu create alchemy now? She describes her current work – coaching, writing and speaking – as being formed in the embers of flames. Knowing the loneliness of survival work, Tamu resolutely creates and values both self-worth and community, creating a matriarchal ecosystem rather than a hierarchical survival system. She uses her extensive training in social work and coaching to help people find their own strength, meet their own needs, then working together, she creates a culture around her work of embodied hope, trust and co-regulation.

Healing-centred work recognizes the importance of regulation. It encourages disruption of the rules and laws of 'power over' and works with our bodies and minds to regulate our nervous systems and internal experience. Regulation is an activism found in care. But co-regulation? Tamu speaks about the power we can only find with others, the depth of connection we can only feel when we are willing to meet our own needs first then work together to meet the needs of the group. This power dynamic feels different, one that Tamu has evolved outside of statutory systems and shaped her powerful work around. I wonder how co-regulation could be embedded through systemic change, threaded through workplaces.

Tamu no longer has to fight a system to prove her worth. Instead, she is showing us what is possible. On her own terms and for the benefit of all working women, she advocates for exquisite rest, sumptuous joy and self-liberation. Tend to yourself, then the group, and create the power to mend society. And that is exactly what social justice work needs to see.

www.livethreesixty.com/

◯ Reflective practice: Record it

What is it?

Recording visually is a way to describe your journey and picture your growth. It's a reflective activity that transforms abstract ideas into a tangible representation of your path. Find some big paper, brown parcel paper works well, and gather pens and crayons. I love oil pastels for the imperfect, bright shapes they create. You'll need different colours.

How do I do it?

Think about your time spent in these pages and draw a plant for each seed of information that's taken root. Label these with words to remind you. Create a space in your garden for pauses and reflection; maybe some woods or a pool. Write about your experiences and findings. Draw a path through the space and add any landmark choices or shifts in your thinking. Spend time drawing, playing with colour, filling the garden. Thank your inner critic if it starts judging and instead turn towards your inner joy by choosing a bright colour or playful shape.

What next?

Your garden map is a vibrant addition to your collection, joining your Invitation, Quest Notes, Dream Collage and Symbol. Use it as a joyful reminder of your growth and display the visual story of your journey.

5

Doorway five: Your power

It's time to step through the courtyard door again. This time it feels less risky. You can return to this building whenever you want. The next space that you will move into is one where you matter, where your energy and ideas focus to create your own unique power. There are more people outside. Some will walk with you on this journey, others will feel further away.

You are going to tread new pathways, new ways to create change, paths forged by healing not pain. You have your life and learning to draw on and your passion and power activated.

Open the door.

Cascade: A poem for activation

Glorious action.
Move me on.
Fast jump forward, propelled from bed.
Move the needle and the thread.
Glorious action.
Feel and think up.

Emotion, wonder, giving do a pep.
Root in awe, find chosen step.

Glorious action.
Cause in motion now.
Compelling on, speed is your fall.
Avoid pain, slow down your call.

Glorious action.
I see you.
Valid, valuable but not alone.
Bring your whole, vulnerability shown.

By Kerry Tottingham

Poetry

Dotted through this book are poems I wrote to celebrate and acknowledge different stages of movement, change and transformation.

Writing poems is an immediate, creative expression that comes to me in a rush sometimes. I love the flow of the words tumbling onto the page and the crafting and tinkering that comes after. The reading aloud that gives me the dashes of grammar and full feeling in my stomach. This poem was a dance in words about the force and impact of action, the buzz and progression it brings. I think of action as not only a physical movement but also a catalyst for change and progress. Something that comes from a person but creates ripples around them. While writing the poem I was thinking about overcoming adversity, facing challenges and living with a forward-moving approach, feeling and thought, and action in motion.

When I am unhappy or in pain, the idea of being propelled into a different place is tantalizing and addictive. The rush of action, in both small and significant ways, compels me and sometimes sweeps me up. The uncomfortable contrast I feel between the positive momentum of action and the stagnation of stillness or hesitation came up in the poetry writing. The 'stillness of dread' is a feeling I can conjure up easily and is still the dark force that propels me when my action comes from an unhealthy place.

As we have explored in the previous chapters, there is a shadow side to feeling, thinking and action. Without reflection, these states can be blinkered and even replicate the problems that we are trying to overcome, resulting in a whirlwind of repeated mistakes and cycles of chaos. Poetry, and art in all its forms, offer a way to explore both the light and the shade. Art can be found in the way you express yourself and in activities you find meaning in; it doesn't have to be visual or written. And just like rest, nourishment, making space to 'be' and tending to our needs, art is essential. Audre Lorde, feminist poet and activist who dedicated her life to confronting injustice, said: 'Poetry is not a luxury. It is a vital necessity of our existence. It forms the quality of the light within which we predicate our hopes and dreams toward survival and change.'

We need to get comfortable with a rhythm of movement and reflection, go and pause, moving in and through light and shade and use art and poetry (or whatever expression works for you) to create a cyclical practice of doing something. Then, pausing to reflect (think and feel) on the outcomes, learnings, opportunities, mistakes and potential means we can continuously learn, refine, adapt and change. Many innovation methodologies that we can use for social change are built on a poetic rhythm. As we have explored, design thinking is a practice of divergent thinking, which means exploring a wide range of possibilities, generating numerous ideas and considering various perspectives (neurodivergence can be super useful in design thinking). This is followed by convergent thinking, narrowing down options, selecting the best ideas, working out what matters and focusing on a specific solution. In nature, there is action in the growth of spring and summer, and reflection in the closing down of autumn and stillness of winter – another poetic cycle.

When we start looking, movement and reflection patterns show up everywhere: in education, in research, in exercise, in technology progression, in crisis management, in trauma-informed practice, in social change work. Sometimes a situation calls for action, other times we need reflection. We can write new poetry every day on this quest, finding power in both glorious action and daring reflection.

Desire paths

We are creating new habits, ways of doing things, pathways to change, desire paths. With these new habits we are not always following routes set by organizations or following tracks that have been established by the people who have gone before us. Sometimes the pathways that we walk along have been created for other people. For example, the 9am–5pm route to getting work done only works for a small number of people. An organization that only values 9am–5pm working will benefit that small minority, creating inequality for anyone who needs or wants an alternative route.

If we have experienced burnout, we might notice that our well-trodden work path connects overwork with validation or productivity with self-esteem. This is a very common and hugely damaging problem in the post-covid world. The conditioning that precedes burnout makes it challenging to find alternative routes (i.e. other than overproduction) to getting work done, which also means our need for meaning. In *How to Do Nothing: Resisting the Attention Economy* Jenny Odell explains: 'Our very idea of productivity is premised on the idea of producing something new, whereas we do not tend to see maintenance and care as productive in the same way.' The book is a call to reclaim our time, attention and sense of purpose from the toxic productivity that commodifies every moment of our lives. She says stopping is an act of resistance and renewal. Paradoxically, I bought this book when I could do nothing due to my health condition, but my motivation for buying it was to feel like I was doing something! It took a few reads for the radical message of the book to sink in.

In 2024, A Brilliant Thing CIC was preparing to take August off. This is a rhythm we have adopted to enable the people who work with us to focus on personal and family tending and nourishment. This was a radical act in itself in a society obsessed with always being 'on' and a sector where scarcity is often the driving force, but we had done this each summer and were confident in its benefits outweighing any negative impacts. However, the nagging downside to this act was returning to a huge inbox and the temptation to slip into that inbox during our break was sometimes too compelling. We were setting ourselves up for stress later and a background hum of worry to follow us around all summer. So we decided to do something about it.

Because our clients and partners were well set up for us taking a break, our communication and planning before the break was excellent. We knew from past experience that most of this huge inbox would be emails we were copied into, and information that would be out of date by the time we got back. We also knew there might be a few opportunities mixed in there, and there could be an urgent request or time critical need. We decided to delete all emails that we received during August and not read any, returning to work in September with an empty inbox.

When we told people about this there was quite a bit of emotion, envy, fear, judgement, avoidance and accusations but also wonder, joy, celebration, gratitude and eyes lighting up. We were not reckless with this choice. Clients had details and clear communication beforehand and check-in meetings were booked in for September. Our social media paused with clear and visual explanations of our choices. We recorded some podcasts to go out over the summer sharing ideas for creative rest and we crafted a thoughtful auto-reply to any emails, even offering a phone number if anything really was urgent, trusting others to make careful decisions on whether they used this number.

Not every job or work situation allows for a long break or for you to take the option of deleting emails (though advocate for this if you can, it's brilliant!). But everyone should take breaks from work and you can certainly set yourself up for calmer returns to work.

Here are some of the ways we prepared for the break that you might like to try:

- Early notification to those we work with.
- Prepare and set up automated processes.
- Clear communication across all channels about why it's important to take the break.
- Schedule ahead to help shake off any guilt.
- Set up for a smooth return (to avoid the 'back to work' feeling!).

This idea really landed. We returned feeling calm and nourished. We received messages from people saying they had put a note in their diary to email again on our return. People spoke to us about how they had changed how they manage team absences and holidays. Instead of copying people into emails or messaging when they know people are away, they save information in one document to share with the person on their return. The best thing was a few months later when we were on the receiving end of others' auto-response emails explaining that they were doing the same!

This ripple effect of people being inspired and changing their own behaviour was brilliant and gave us evidence of the importance of visibly creating new ways of doing things that align with the Healing-Centred Design principles. The ways of doing things that we are conditioned for in society can be dangerous. Following the crowd, blindly, will lead to more pain. A different way of doing things is to create desire paths.

What are desire paths?

In Japan, urban planners leave parks without walkways for a few months, adding landscaped paths that follow the natural tracks made by people at a later date. In Finland, officials visit public spaces just after a snowfall to see where they should create routes.

Desire paths emerge when we repeatedly follow an unmarked track, creating a groove in the landscape that signals a different way. Similarly, we can create new paths to getting impactful, meaningful work done, while also meeting our physical, emotional and experiential needs. Here's how.

Step 1: Notice your needs

We often forget that, as humans, we require support to thrive, develop and create brilliant things in the world. The first step to creating a new desire path is to notice when your body and mind are signalling support needs. You might notice:

- **Increased stress**: Feeling overwhelmed or anxious? Pain, twitchy muscles, headaches? Pay attention to the messages your body is sending. Acknowledge physical and sensory triggers.
- **Changes in momentum**: An unexplained decline in productivity might indicate a need for a fresh perspective or a helping hand. Notice where your momentum and rhythm feels out of balance.
- **Isolation or unfulfilling connection**: Feeling disconnected from colleagues can lead to loneliness and undervaluation. Sometimes this is because you feel out of alignment with your own values. Notice where you feel connection in your life, notice when you feel connected to yourself. Where are the gaps?
- **Burnout signals**: Exhaustion, irritability and reduced enthusiasm are signs of burnout. Create mindful pauses throughout your day for gentle reflection.

- **Unresolved challenges**: Avoiding unresolved obstacles drains your energy. Instead, notice how you could work through challenges with the support you need to avoid isolation and procrastination.

Step 2: Consider the journey

We are creating a journey along this new path, one that replenishes us while we create impactful work.

Now you know your support needs, here are some prompts to ponder:

- **Starting point**: Reflect on where you currently stand in your journey towards impactful work. What is happening around you? What habits or beliefs are holding you back?
- **Moving along the path**: Identify small steps you can take to adapt your approach to work and self-care. Embrace breaks, set boundaries and practise self-compassion.
- **Support along the way**: Determine the support you require to stay on your desired path. Seek replenishment, consider your physical needs and strengthen social connections. Explore coaching, mentoring or group support.
- **The destination**: Clarify what impactful work means to you. How will you know when you have arrived? What will you feel like at the end? What needs will have been met? Set tangible goals and track your progress.

Power structures

Choosing our own path is empowering. Notice how you feel about power now. It might be more layered and complex or maybe you are starting to embody your personal power. Can you see and feel collective power as an antidote to pain in ourselves and in the world? Empowerment can awaken, swirl in us, create an aura, be expressed beautifully through our eyes, shared through our words, our actions. But power can also cause harm, and if we have experienced that harm it can be very hard to allow our own inner power to rise.

People who work against privilege, entitlement and injustice often reject power or even fear it. If we summon up that inner power (that we all secretly know is there), we worry we might inflict, cause harm, say or do things that wield our power like a blunt hammer. Fearing power allows more space for people who feel they are owed or deserve power to snatch it away. But just like lasting damage isn't the inevitable outcome of trauma, harm isn't the inevitable outcome of power – power can be something quite different. If used in healing-centred ways, we can channel power for good. Power structures and unjust systems can be replaced. We can build our own power structures, not cathedrals of privilege or towers of oppression but villages of healing, walkways and bridges of connection, nurturing homes and places that contain creativity, wells of ideas, pools holding vulnerability and hope.

The power structures we see in society are often hierarchical ways of organizing and distributing power, wealth and privilege. The concentrated wealth in many societies creates damaging systems and constructs divisions. When we believe power is scarce, finite and rare, the ways we organize builds walls of influence and uses windows into others' lives to show what might happen if we step out of line. Control, rigid organizing, threats of explosion, unless we follow fixed rules. Even if we think there is plenty of power to go around, sometimes our conditioning tells us only some people deserve power, while others would be dangerous with it or waste it or be careless and burn down our lives.

But what if we believed power was abundant? What if we didn't hold it like a cautious flame in a fragile glass or use it to spotlight and interrogate? What if we instead allowed its power to glow and fill the room? Warm, healing, soothing, crystallizing, gleaming power. What if we were not afraid of power and knew that each person had endless wells to draw from, many forms of power ebbing and flowing, cycling like moonlight, starlight, sunlight? Could this kind of power be channelled like light? Allowed to flow around and over and between, illuminating the dark and difficult corners, lighting spaces with energy and possibility? We could create new structures to channel power, new spaces to fill up, rivers of power flowing between people, reciprocal structures that contribute to and benefit the landscape.

What could these channelling power structures look like? Maybe a set of practices, principles or evocations. The walls might be made of the soft clay of conversation rather than rules that are impenetrable like stone. The warm clay marked with fingerprints and hands gently nudging and forming, reforming as power moves through. Channelled and concentrated and beaming. If this healing power rose up, strengthened with structure, gathered its energy to match the murky power of pain, what would happen? Imagine these entities and you might assume a fight. 'I am as powerful as you, now I can drown out your shadows!' 'You can never light me, I will smother your glow with nightmares!' and so on, and so on, until everything was gone except chaos.

But I don't think that is what would happen. Because healing power would not be concerned with the fight. She'd be flowing around the roots, in the grasses like a breeze. She'd be healing and touching and gently soothing the pain left by oppression, whispering radical thoughts, 'Things can be different'. She'd be singing in your slumber a low, soft, comforting hum, waking other gifts up: imagination, intuition, ideas nurtured. Healing power wouldn't be rallying for a fight, she'd be gathering the scattered, forgotten and disregarded parts that pain split off from you. Your confidence, your inner knowing, your self-love, your needs, gathered and returned to you with a steady gaze.

Pain would roil and squirm and beat its chest, jabbing you with blows as you sleep, ripping through muscles and shoving you to wake up. But you wouldn't stir. You are in a dance with healing, each jab of pain a reminder of your beautiful tender parts and a nudge to place attention there. Eventually pain would roll away, retreating with a slump in a murky mood. Huffing that it didn't need you anyway, you are a lost cause. Disappearing into the gloom, dragging its lumpen stone walls, graffitied with rules, and broken windows with no views, away.

And healing power continues her breeze, blowing through shadows and stirring up clouds of change. She flows in you, around you, through you. At once there and then past, her presence both clear and ephemeral. You can't catch her, confine her to a box or a castle, but she can be channelled, drawn in, invited.

Choice, intention, compassion

Form follows choice, connection follows intention and tolerance follows compassion. Read this slowly! Things that are made are representations of the choices of the maker. Connections happen most often when we are intentionally open. Being tolerant, accepting and understanding is far more possible when we are compassionate with ourselves and with others.

If we are designing a party, we need to know its purpose before we craft the invite, decorate the room and choose the ideas index. The form of the party is shaped by the choices we make about its purpose; a wedding party might look and feel very different from a children's birthday party. If we are designing ways to create collective power, create connection between different groups of people and build relationships, being clear on our intention and sharing this openly will start to build trust and understanding of the work you hope to do.

If we want to come to terms with chronic pain, accept the parts of us that are tender and put down the tug of war rope between ourselves and our pain, we can begin with compassion for our hurting selves, our coping selves and our healing selves.

The change work we are involved in takes shape and finds its form when connection and tolerance are present. Shaping and forming our change work is like moulding clay, shaping with skill and deft touch, making mistakes and reshaping, experimenting with marks and tools, patterning surfaces and texturizing in layers. The potter has infinite possibilities with a hunk of clay, something useful, beautiful, or functional or sculptural could be created; multiple, similar objects could be shaped or a collection of characterful squat pots could follow a swan-like vase. The potter makes choices based on purpose, materials available, time and imagination. These choices, like an invisible hand, forming the outcome.

Connection can happen in moments or last lifetimes. Making connections, discovering shared experiences or perspectives or tastes can be foundational for friendship, communities and memory making.

Less is written, however, about disconnecting with care and empathy. The term 'conscious uncoupling' was splashed across headlines in 2014 when actress Gwyneth Paltrow and musician Chris Martin described their mindful separation. They talked about mutual respect, co-parenting and personal growth rather than animosity or conflict, but the reaction I remember was one of ridicule. I think we are so conditioned to be averse to endings that we can't imagine one without a fight. I was reminded of this term, conscious uncoupling, recently when a relationship with a friend felt heavy and I realized the friendship had run its course. I wanted to write a letter intending to 'consciously uncouple', but when I spoke with others about this, the first reaction was often advice to let things fizzle out. I did, but I'm not sure that was the right choice for me. Before Gwyneth and Chris, the term had deeper roots in psychology and therapy and describes approaching the end of a relationship with awareness, intentionality and emotional maturity. Rather than viewing separation as a failure or a destructive process, it highlights the potential for personal transformation, healing and positive outcomes for both individuals involved. I haven't written the letter yet, but my intention is to be open to communicate a clear and compassionate ending. Just setting this intention allows my body to let go of some of the tension around this relationship.

Tolerance is another term society struggles with. It's much easier to grab attention with ultimatums and rigid perspectives. The tolerance we need for change doesn't mean accepting the status quo or being passive. Tolerance here is about working with people, ideas or structures that you might not necessarily agree with or support. I recently worked with a client who was so opposed to working with decision makers that they were missing opportunities for constructive collaboration. Building their tolerance involved taking small risks into the unknown to build awareness and confidence and understanding where their tolerance edges were. This involved coaching them to use compassionate language as they described their own feelings around the situation, gentling nudging away from judgement to cultivate empathy, patience and understanding towards themselves then others, while clearly communicating needs and boundaries. We all have a stubborn, inner child that digs her heels in and refuses to budge when there is something she doesn't like, but change this way can take longer and feel harder. Of course, tolerance has edges too. Sometimes a refusal is needed when a line is crossed or our position needs to be understood. In fact, when we spend time, most of our time, working and living within a channel of tolerance, we make an even bigger statement when we declare an edge (like the deleting emails action we took in the desire paths section).

These phrases can be the nudges you need as you move along your change journey:

- **Form follows choice**: The shape and direction of our lives are influenced by the decisions we make. Our actions, behaviours and experiences are shaped by the choices we consciously or unconsciously make and that manifest our reality.
- **Connection follows intention**: Our intentions guide meaningful connections with others. When we approach interactions with genuine intentions of understanding, empathy and connection, we create the foundation for authentic relationships and mutual understanding.
- **Tolerance follows compassion**: Tolerance towards others stems from a place of compassion and empathy and knowing our own edges. When we cultivate compassion for others and seek to understand their perspectives, we naturally become more tolerant of differences and diversity.

Multiple sources of power

Choice, connection and compassion. All powers we can cultivate, but where does this power live? We often use image cards at the beginning of group sessions in an activity called 'What lives in this team?' We display the images around the room and ask everyone to pick one that tells us something about themselves. We notice how people choose the cards – decisively, with care, quickly, paying attention to others' choices – and reflect with the group what helped them choose, then invite everyone to share their card and meaning. We identify strengths, commonalities, tensions and ideas, displaying the chosen cards on the wall or centre of the table. This display stays up for the remainder of the session, helping people remember and draw on what came up during this exercise.

When we identify strengths within ourselves, we become empowered. When we share power with others, we hold collective power. Sometimes people feel a compulsion to give away power in reaction to others taking too much power, to avoid getting into bed with the oppression of unwieldy political power, discriminating financial power or extractive resources power.

But power and privilege are not the same thing. Removing the frame of privilege from power, power becomes the ability to change, resource, grow and develop. I considered this on a dim January day, walking in the wet woods near my house, icy liquid running off all surfaces. Moss sodden and water cleaving clay rivulets, feeding the river, I considered the power of nature. The force of a river, the wave of change spring brings, the human body channelling its power to grow another human or fight a cancer. In nature, power helps the ecosystem adapt and thrive and shapes the environment. In physics, power is represented in an equation, where power equals work over time:

- P is power.
- W is the work done or energy transferred.
- T is the time taken.

Physics shows power as an indicator; it tells us how fast something is happening or how quickly energy is being used or produced. So, the power of a waterfall is a measure of how fast it's transferring gravity, or 'potential' energy into kinetic, or 'active' energy, pounding the rocks below and moving the water along the river (this is the 'work'). The speed, the potential, the activity and the work, all valuable elements of the waterfall, together creating power.

But the power of a waterfall isn't just in the kinetic energy transfer, it's the beauty of the water finding its way through the crevices, sculpting the rock and the play of light and sound as the liquid tumbles, crashes, pools and surges.

There are many types of power, from healing power to information power. Wayfinding Inc. have identified 30 types of power at work and developed a Power Landscape, including power found in personal wellbeing, relationships and intimacy, organizational transformation, society and nature, and ceremony and meaning. In *A New Weave of Power, People and Politics: The Action Guide for Advocacy and Citizen Participation* by Lisa VeneKlasen and Valerie Miller, power is represented in four quadrants:

- **Power over**: Taking power away from another and using for own gain.
- **Power with**: Collective strength, power between us.
- **Power to**: Potential to shape our life and world.
- **Power within**: Belief that, wherever we start from, we can all make a difference.

This multidimensional understanding of power gives us language to reclaim power. Power is not bad. Power can be used in different ways. A powerful force has energy that can change things; when we need social change, when we need to undo, heal and create new where oppression, inequality and pain lies. When pain is caused by power over, then power with, power to and power within can form an alliance – a power trio. Nourishing the trio, within, without, between, creating an ecosystem of powerful transformation.

Ecosystem

Complexity and mutual power is beautifully demonstrated by ecosystems in nature. Life Forest is an exercise that you can use to articulate self-identity within a connected system and is a useful reflection tool for personal development that can also be applied to understand deeper meanings within a project or organization. You start with a single tree, the roots, branches and leaves becoming visual metaphors for your experiences. To make sense of complex issues like transforming pain into power, this tree needs to be seen as part of an intricate ecosystem: a forest. The Life Forest exercise uses the metaphor of a rich and layered forest to describe existence in communities, societies and the multiple circumstances that impact on our lives. You can find a template for this exercise on our website www.brilliantthing.co.uk/make

Some of these complexities we can influence, others seem harder to change. Our work too exists within a multilayered environment. If you chose a specific event in your work life and traced all the micro events leading up to that point, you would have created an ecosystem involving many people, situations, places and conditions. Every action is powerful, each causes a reaction, a ripple of consequences and impacts.

No entity understands this better than a forest. A forest is an area of land covered in trees, plants, thriving nature and regeneration. Forests across the globe provide an ecosystem that supports humanity by providing the air we breathe and creating life-giving habitats. Forests are interconnected; each tree, plant, animal and insect plays a role that contributes to the forest's survival. Trees share water and nutrients through underground root networks, and also use them to communicate, sending messages about environmental changes, signalling warnings and nurturing new plants. This cooperation and collaboration spans different species and creates a successful and diverse forest. *Finding the Mother Tree: Uncovering the Wisdom and Intelligence of the Forest* by Suzanne Simard describes this interwoven forest life in awe inspiring and touching detail. If identity (personal or organizational) can be described through a tree metaphor, what can we learn about our work and our society through a forest metaphor?

Characteristics of a 'successful' forest

Seasonal variation

- Recognize the seasonal patterns within your life. These might be community events, holidays, back to school time, etc.
- Free write in your journal, describing how these impact on you and what you could change. Consider which seasonal events or phases align with your work.
- Spend 30 minutes grouping all your activities under seasonal headings. Is there a clear seasonal focus? Could you amplify this?

Deciduous and evergreen mix

- Make a list of the things that are constants in your life. These might be people, feelings, living environment, etc. Make another list of things that come and go.
- Do you need to strengthen evergreen (constant) elements in your life or focus on letting some elements go so they can return at another time?
- Consider the time and energy that you spend on core and recurrent activities compared to the benefits that these each bring.
- Have a conversation with your team or a friend about this. Do you need to adjust the balance?

Canopy for protection

- When we are vulnerable, we need protection. Sometimes this becomes a habit or a way of being, and we avoid risk and uncertainty. Brene Brown describes how 'Vulnerability is the birthplace of love, belonging, joy, courage, empathy, and creativity.'
- Consider the level of risk you allow into your life. Do you need to cultivate or prune your canopy?
- Maslow's hierarchy of needs describes tiers of needs that must be met for a person to develop into the best version of themselves.
- Try creating a hierarchy of needs for your work to develop into the best version of itself. What do you learn?

Habitats for creatures

- Brainstorm the word 'collaboration', adding notes on where you 'collaborate' in your life and what it feels like. In a different colour, add in the things that help collaboration to happen.
- Use a highlighter pen to identify any spaces, relationships or ideas on your brainstorm that you could help to blossom by creating conditions that they can thrive in.
- Add branches to each of these conditions and note what things support these. Keep repeating until you identify the underlying things that you need for this area of work to thrive.

Fertile ground

- How do you nurture yourself?
- How do you invest in your work?
- How can you do more of this?

Relationships between flora and fauna

- Using the Life Forest activity, identify your 'fruits'. What abundance do you hold that you could share? You may have abundant ideas, time or skills.
- Reflect on how you could share this value in more generous ways to cultivate reciprocal relationships.

These ideas provide inspiration for personal development and act as prompts to encourage a way of thinking, feeling and acting as part of a bigger, collaborative, powerful ecosystem. This collective power creates an environment where we each create positive ripples of impact and contribute to a collective, thriving experience.

Magnetic support

This work needs support. Multifaceted, multilayered, adaptable, flexible, expansive, magnetic support. Personal, collective or public social change needs at least double the support you think it does.

To tell my story of pain and use it to inspire change, I need support to craft my story, emotional support as I relive my story, listening support, supportive time and space afterwards. To dismantle inequality in organizations, I need support from decision makers to be open minded to listen to the impact of their systems and processes. Support during workshops to tackle big emotive topics safely. Support for the change process and the people navigating it. Support to share information across teams and communicate changes and impacts. To shift how society sees people who have experienced pain, from damaged and needing to be fixed, to resilient people embodying the strength to contribute, create and use transformational power, I need support from the people closest to me and support from people I have never met.

Double, triple, quadruple support

Currently, I am part of a coaching community. I see a personal coach, a business coach and a therapist. I have a personal reflective practice and offer reflective practice spaces within all The Brilliant Club. Our development programme offers how to learn and apply Healing-Centred Design. My husband generously offers me Reiki alongside reciprocal emotional space and practical support. I am under the medical care of two consultants and appreciate the remedies from my mother-in-law who is a homeopath. Then there are the supportive wellbeing practices I try to sustain: exercise, meal prep, being outside, time away from screens, time blocking, many baths! This might all seem excessive. My internal conditioning is scoffing as I write this list of support. What a millennial! So needy! Self-obsessed! But there is a quieter voice too. She says, you are doing big things, and have big barriers, so you need big support.

We all need a mix of support: doing things on our own, relying on each other and working together. Independent, interconnected and collaborative support build our strength and build supportive communities where we can create collectively. Support is magnetic – create a supportive practice in your life and it will draw in more of what you want and need. Albert Bandura's Social Learning Theory explains that people learn from observing others and the consequences of their actions. 'Reciprocal Determinism' is a key aspect of this theory and describes how people and their environment mutually influence each other and supports the idea that cultivating support can create a magnetic effect.

Our fridge door was a mess of holiday magnets, trapping reminders and out-of-date vouchers. A school trip to Flamingo Land holding a grubby photo and our honeymoon trip to Malta pinning a recipe card, nestled amongst various never-used bottle opener magnets with emotional attachment. Reorganizing my fridge door was never a priority, but on a rainy Saturday I needed a pottering job to distract me and the fridge door trumped the Tupperware cupboard! I placed our memories back in a pleasing order, binned the out-of-date reminders, gathered the recipes together and rescued a photo to frame. It became a place to pause and smile before retrieving the milk.

One of the only magnets that wasn't a place memento had a quote on it. 'Big thinking precedes great achievement' by Wilfred Peterson. Procrastinating about throwing out years old children's artwork, I googled and found out that Peterson was an American author who wrote articles about love, peaceful thinking and healthy living, with a focus on personal responsibility and supporting self-improvement. I found out his words had legacy. He wrote the most frequently recited English-language wedding poem and his inspirational essays were made into greeting cards and gifts popular in Hallmark stores for decades. Wilfred wasn't afraid of support. In fact, he proclaimed it and marketed it!

Curating powerful support

You might need different types of support: a cleaner, babysitting, time with your hands in the soil, a printer that works (!), flexible hours at work, mending, borrowing, learning, listening, mentoring, tending. Think expansively and support yourself as much as you are able to. Put plans in motion for bigger support when time or money allows. Save for it, ask the universe for it, request from people around you or reach out online. Curating and tailoring your support might involve transactions, paying for it, time swaps with friends, accessing free support from charities or online, asking others how they gain support, gaining insight and finding wisdom.

What if we displayed the support we benefit from like magnets on a fridge door, collected and shared symbols of the helpful support we have received; the supportive tools and reminders. Could we create a collective collage of support like a fridge door adorned with memories and messages? By normalizing the support we all need, identifying where the support gaps are and where we need to change the support we receive, we can reduce the divide between the person who needs help and the person helping – we can equalize. By talking about support, sharing the coaching, showing others how and where we receive support, we can encourage others to view support as a right not an add-on – an essential need.

The Plunge

Near me there is a wood with a stream and waterfalls. The paths turn into streams in the winter and the earth is covered with a bluebell carpet in spring. Underneath one rocky waterfall is a deep pool; it's known locally as The Plunge. To find The Plunge, you have to visit the village of Edenfield, walk down Plunge Lane to the ruins of Plunge Mill and wind through Dearden Woods. These charming names set the scene and The Plunge always feels like a secret gem to be discovered. There is something about depth that tells me the word 'plunge' is evocative. Now feels like the time for depth, deep change work, finding wisdom and connection that comes with immersing.

We hear 'I'm just conscious of time', 'We have a packed agenda', 'Let's take that offline'. Our current working practices rarely allow for depth, deep listening, immersion. But we soak up the culture of productivity, goal setting and achievement. Success seeming binary, you win or you don't, and reductive media reinforces the idea that complex issues can be solved with a vote, a decision or a reactionary policy. Yet we know complex issues of pain, transformation and equitable collective power require depth, breadth and choices to enable deep-rooted change.

Depth can be found with an 'obsession', something that receives consistent, focused attention. This might be an obsession with understanding an experience or it could be an obsession with change or an obsession with your values. Organizations who intentionally focus on depth might employ a deep democracy approach, where all voices and experiences are heard and understood to support systemic change. Organizations can oppose a culture of quick fixes, reactive mistakes and sticking plasters and create the benefits of depth (connection, trust, loyalty, wellbeing, innovation) by creating more depth to their work.

The depth of our emotional health, our inner resources and our mindset determines our resilience, our capacity and our ideas. When my well is shallow, I am less emotionally available. My tolerance lowers, I can feel apathy. When I focus on depth, by honouring my core needs, rest, nutrition, water nurturing play, learning, creativity and surrounding myself with difference – experiences, people, ideas – I grow and take up space to be fully, deeply me.

Plunge deep

You might spend some time on the edge before you plunge deep. I had a coaching session with 'Real You, Real Money' coach and podcaster Ray Dodd when I was wavering at the edge of a big work-life transition. Money scarcity had been one of my fears and so to support me through this move I had found the most non-capitalist money coach I could on the internet to work with! The feedback I had received about leaving my job had been quite overwhelming and I had a Word document of copied and pasted emails that I couldn't quite bring myself to read. Though I was sure of the decision, I was afraid that reading people's feedback would make me question if the right time was now, or even worse question if I was 'selling out', even though I *knew* this path I have chosen wasn't going to be a walk in the park.

Ray invited me to draw a stick version of myself at the top of a page and underneath write all the qualities that make me uniquely me. She asked me to list all the things I keep with me no matter what job or situation I am in. Personal qualities, skills, capabilities, I was encouraged to keep adding to the list until it felt complete. She showed me through this list what 'dropped' beneath me, the depth of me, the roots. As I plunged down, lengthening my list, I felt a deep sense of security – here I am, my intuition, my imagination, my tenderness, all here in the depths.

It was such a helpful, affirming session, and after letting the reflections sink in I had another idea. Working alone this time, I drew the same stick version of me at the bottom of the opposite page. I then slowly read through the feedback I had received, noting down all the qualities, skills and abilities mentioned. These were things that people see, that had 'risen' out of me. The rise illuminated others' perceptions of me, sharing as much about them as what they saw and felt in me. Comparing the lists there were some similarities, qualities that felt aligned internally and externally. But there were also some that were hidden – internal qualities that I didn't let rise at work. I realized that these were exactly the qualities that I wanted to integrate into the next phase of my work life. Have a go at this activity. What hidden qualities are in your depths, and is it time for them to emerge?

Transformation Treasure Box

Have you ever had a collection? Spoons or thimbles or pages of stamps? As a child, I collected handfuls of beach glass and strung multiple shells with holes on twine. I collected seeds in the garden and gathered buttons like colourful jewels. I collected objects alongside emotions, feeling all the feels and categorizing experiences. I organized holiday mementos in scrapbooks and beads in matchboxes. I stowed experiences away in boxes, shutting away reminders and wrapping up parcels of things I wanted to keep for myself and creating nests for particularly special findings. There was a magical-ness in collecting, organizing, wrapping, boxing, hiding away and displaying.

I feel this magical-ness when I'm pottering, arranging, curating objects and emotions. Moving into a new house after years of saving and wishing opens an almost overwhelming opportunity for magical collecting and curating. Writing this book has been a practice of organizing and arranging, experiences, thoughts and emotions, gathering skills and tools, crafts and utensils for change.

The collection of creative expressions and exercises that you have been invited to create and complete in these pages become your own Transformation Treasure Box. A collection of artifacts, ways of thinking, explorations, imaginings, all supporting you. You can look back on your collection and see the intricacies and multiplicities of transformation. Keep your Transformation Treasure Box safe. I recommend a special box or bag or shelf to keep your collection together. Enjoy the ritual of gathering and arranging these items, creating space in your home and mind for this work to continue.

To complete this journey we have the Restructure Ritual, an ending exercise using drawing and doodling that offers a way to recreate and move on. You can use this ritual again and again as you move through the multiple beginnings and endings, doorways and thresholds that are ahead of you.

Threshold: Healing-Centred Design framework, pass it on

The Healing-Centred Design framework guides transformation from pain to power and creates a lightness of energy, inspiration, connection and possibility to fuel momentum. Who in your life can you gift these qualities to? Whose light do you want to see shine? How can you continue the momentum of healing-centred transformation?

Visit www.brilliantthing.co.uk/give and you'll find a token you can pass on.

Healing-Centred Design Framework

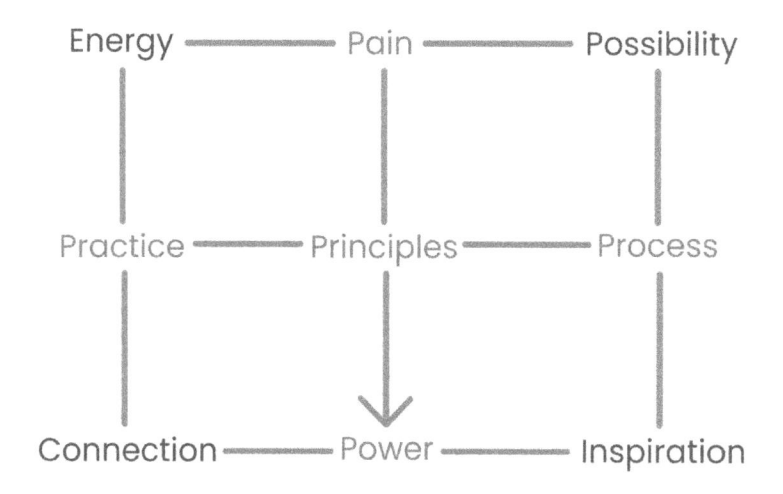

```
Energy ──────── Pain ──────── Possibility
  │              │              │
  │              │              │
Practice ──── Principles ──── Process
  │              │              │
  │              ▼              │
Connection ──── Power ──────── Inspiration
```

Case study: Kirstie Henderson, founder of Brave Day

Kirstie Henderson, founder of Brave Day, is a creative director, filmmaker and storyteller. Her films highlight resilience, amplify marginalized voices and inspire change through powerful, authentic storytelling. Kirstie lives with ulcerative colitis, a health condition that has shaped how she works.

Reflecting on pain, Kirstie recognizes the depths and breadths of painful experiences

– her own physical pain a reaction to the emotional pain that she can't remember living without. Emotional pain hiding in the body. The body and mind finding all the ways to avoid and contain pain and shaping herself around others' pain without ever talking about it.

Yet pain radiated. Travelling around the world, solo adventuring, meeting people and seeing places to stretch, grow and experience. This was supposed to be freedom for Kirstie. But on her return, the yearning to expand was met with sudden illness and eventually a chronic health diagnosis. Just like the doors were closed around mental health conversations, physical health issues were not welcomed. She had to cope and carry on and landed in the corporate world. Events and communication companies were high paced, stressful environments. Working under the pressure of unsupportive systems and ways of working, Kirstie still progressed. Promotions and achievements beaming an outward success, while her body battled hidden illness.

And then an opportunity arrived, part forced, part taken willingly. This opportunity needed courage to seize it. Kirstie left her job to go freelance and Brave Day emerged. Kirstie describes Brave Day as a call to action. A call to explore bravery, to make films about people progressing through life. Stories of challenges and overcoming adversity, watching real people living pain and beauty-filled, creative lives. Films about the experience of addiction captured in dance, poetry exploring the experience of injustice, music, art and words layered with shadow and light.

Through Kirstie's work you can see a fascination with the internal and external experiences of stress, pain, injustice and liberation radiating throughout. Brave Day is a social enterprise but has also become her daily practice taken in small actions. Brave choices to seek learning experiences, find inspiring people, stretch outside of herself. When times are darker, she can reach for people, be touched by the moments of transformation she films, immerse in learning and gentle creative reflection.

Kirstie has not found a pain-free life, or even a life where she is free from all constraints. Instead, she has found a place where she can be herself, where she has courage to stay present alongside pain. Staying with care and attention, filming moments and illuminating stories, embodying the changes she sees and reflecting on the growth she feels. She doesn't hide every bad feeling anymore but recognizes them as tools for personal development.

Life ebbs and flows, painful moments strung into painful years, painful decades. But things transform, fruit and evolve. There is a magnetism in the work Kirstie is being drawn to, work that explores the connection between minds and body, storytelling and creativity with people living with chronic conditions, somatic work that involves seeing, feeling and experiencing. Through reflective practice and being in a community with other justice-led creative people, Kirstie can feel the activist in her rising. There is anger, emotion and power ignited as her work addresses inequality, sharing the art and stories of marginalized experiences. When I spoke with Kirstie for this story, having been a witness and friend for the last ten years, I got goosebumps. Because for the first time I heard her pondering where her character might go next and wonder about putting more of herself into the story.

Maybe the nurturing, accepting, creative, expansive place Kirstie has been searching for through the years is the one she has been making the whole time.

www.braveday.co.uk/

◯ Reflective practice: Draw it out

What is it?

Restructure Ritual is a drawing ritual for completion – a moment to restructure and reframe your journey and express your vision of transformation. Rituals mark the passing of time, creating cairns in our consciousness, elevating moments with symbolic actions. This ritual is an opportunity to recognize the barriers, label the things that have hurt you before and reorganize and restructure how you want your experience to feel going forward. But this isn't a plan or set of actions. This ritual is a shift, a movement, a flow and an expression.

How do I do it?

Wash your hands, clear your space, sip a cool glass of water. You'll need a quiet space and a protected parcel of time. Take some big paper (I like to use a roll of wallpaper lining paper or brown craft paper) and a pen.

Draw a box on one side of your paper. Label this box pain and write inside the things that have conditioned you, kept you stuck, hurt, the rules, expectations and injustices that have shaped how you live. Keep your writing short and factual.

Now draw a house around the box, extending your drawing across the page. Create a house with many rooms, doorways, thresholds and gardens. You can give your house stairways, bookshelves, windows and fireplaces. Use your imagination to doodle and create different spaces that give you generous support.

The doorways in this book led to rooms where we explored mending and tending through principles, processes and practices. We delved into power and transformation. We got to know your depths and wisdom. In the rooms and spaces you have drawn, add some writing – note down things you have found, learned or created in the pages of this book.

This is your house of transformation. Pain is one room in this house, but there are multiple spaces to occupy and discover. This house represents you, and you can choose when and how to open the doors. You can add rooms, you can renovate, rebuild. You can let light circulate in this house, open the doors and let the past become a source of strength, and new rooms become where you transform that pain into power. You can welcome people in to share that beautiful, collective power.

Let this sink in by drawing a path to the house. Make it wind and curve. Now without removing your pencil from the paper, ground the house in its environment. Around the house scribble in grass and plants, water, pebbles and whatever else comes to mind: a pet, a waterfall, a door, a treasure box. Use loose scribbly marks, move the pencil with your whole arm or create tight repeated marks and shapes. Imagine the scribbles are music, keep going even if you feel silly. Enjoy the flow of pencil on paper. Take your scribbles and waves up to the structure. Wind your lines around walls, windows, doors. Add a whisper of smoke from a chimney, a beam of light on the front door.

Notice how you feel.

Invitation to a party

When was the last time you followed in instinct?

In 2023, I wanted to make a product. A Brilliant Thing CIC was a service-based business and we were doing well, lots of interesting projects, a growing network and a feeling that we were making a difference to how people experienced their work. But I wanted a thing, something we could hold in our hands and say, 'We made this.' We started to create a set of artworks and tried to sell these online – only a few sales happened. I wondered if my urge to make something wasn't a work-related urge but something I could just do for myself. So I started making collages. Intricate, imagination-filled collages made with old photos and gathered papers, collected images and neon paints. This was a healing moment for me. Placing photos of childhood me alongside pictures of my own children when they were young. Creating small worlds in paper and colour, exploring themes of lost and found, release and cultivation.

Around the same time I was systematically writing down some of the key concepts, exercises and tools of Healing-Centred Design as we developed the framework. It was in a workshop when I brought along some of my collages to explain an experience that I collided these ideas and The Brilliant Box was born. The Brilliant Box is a development deck of coaching cards with reflective images on one side and development activities on the other. You can use the cards to support self, community, group or organizational development, and there are multiple ways to use them – from card-pulls to spark new ideas to developing a project plan or guiding group work.

When you create a new product you are supposed to test the market – we slightly, naïvely skipped this step! I designed the cards and we invested some money in producing a batch. We launched the boxes in two ways: at a festival event and as a prize for the first three people who signed up to The Brilliant Club, which is our programme to learn and apply Healing-Centred Design.

The festival was glorious, even though it sleeted! We had a stall in a gazebo but made it into a gorgeous warm, light and colour filled space. We invited people in to help create a map representing all the brilliant connections and people at the event. We had joy-filled conversations and sold lots of our boxes (and the artwork that had flopped when we wanted to sell it online!). Following this event, we developed The Brilliant Box Experience, a travelling sideshow that pops up at conferences and events. Imagine a play-box of creative connection activities and free micro-coaching, designed to help people explore unexpected connections, tap into their creativity and contribute and benefit from a DIY 'Asks and Offers' board!

Using The Brilliant Box as a prize is something we now embed in all our launches and hold Parties with Prizes twice a year. For these free events we also buy products for prizes from other social enterprises, charities and small businesses. Some of our favourites include handmade upcycled denim aprons from Maverick Lab in Rochdale and beautifully designed gifts from Arthouse Unlimited, a charity who present the artistic talents of adults with complex neurodiverse and physical support needs.

Caroline Gleaves, Chief Officer of Gorse Hill Studios, an inspirational youth arts charity in Manchester and attendee of a Leadership Development course facilitated by me, won a box and shared:

> I was lucky I won a brilliant, Brillant Box. This perfect package of inspiration has helped me think outside of the box. It's acted as a prompt on how to approach a situation when sometimes we have experience and knowledge and just need that little nudge. It's a reminder of the tools I learned during a course with A Brilliant Thing CIC, to safely collaborate, inspire and care. The possibilities are endless if you just have some lovely visual stimulus for a group discussion, or ways to tackle a day when you are literally stuck.

The instinct to make a thing mattered. Listening to how I felt made more brilliant things happen. I encourage you to feel deep and know brilliant things will happen.

Thank you for spending time in these pages with me. Would you like to stay in touch? We'd love to invite you to the next party with prizes!

Pop onto our mailing list for an invite www.brilliantthing.co.uk/mail

Find us online @abrilliantthing

Appendices

Buy a book to pass on, 10% off token www.brilliantthing.co.uk/give

Healing-Centred Design templates online at www.brilliantthing.co.uk/make

Invitation to a party www.brilliantthing.co.uk/mail

References

Welcome

Chronic pain and injustice statistics
World Health Organization (WHO) (n.d.). *Chronic Pain Prevalence and Global Burden.* Available from: www.who.int [accessed 24 November 2024].

Healing-centred engagement
Ginwright, S. *The Future of Healing: Shifting From Trauma-Informed Care to Healing-Centered Engagement* (2018). Available from: https://ginwright.medium.com [accessed 24 November 2024].

Trauma-informed work
Herman, J.L. *Trauma and Recovery: The Aftermath of Violence—From Domestic Abuse to Political Terror* (1997). New York: Basic Books.

Chapter 1: Doorway one: Pain

It's not that bad
Ginwright, S. *The Future of Healing: Shifting From Trauma-Informed Care to Healing-Centered Engagement* (2018). Available from: https://ginwright.medium.com [accessed 24 November 2024].

National Institute for Health and Care Excellence (NICE), 'Chronic pain (primary and secondary) in over 16s:

assessment of all chronic pain and management of chronic primary pain' in NICE guideline [NG193] (2021). Available from: www.nice.org.uk [accessed 24 November 2024].

Anatomy of pain
Ashar, Y.K., Gordon, A., Schubiner, H., Uipi, D., Knight, D.C., Anderson, S.R., Kross, E. and Wager, T.D. 'Pain Reprocessing Therapy for chronic back pain: A randomized controlled trial' in *JAMA Psychiatry*, 78(12), 1242–1250 (2021). Available from: https://jamanetwork.com [accessed 24 November 2024].

Conditioning
Trust for London and New Policy Institute, *Poverty and Inequality in Kensington and Chelsea* (2017). Available from: www.trustforlondon.org.uk [accessed 24 November 2024].

Restorative practices and social change
Safe Hands and Thinking Minds (n.d.) *Dr Karen Treisman: Trauma-Informed Resources and Frameworks*. Available from: www.safehandsthinkingminds.co.uk [accessed 24 November 2024].

Floods of revolution
Tate (n.d.) 'Assemblage: Art Term' in Tate Glossary. Available from: www.tate.org.uk [accessed 24 November 2024].

Plastic change
University of Colorado, Boulder. 'Mind-body Treatments for Chronic Back Pain' in National Library of Medicine, ClinicalTrials.gov. Available from: https://clinicaltrials.gov/study/NCT03294148

Chapter 2: Doorway two: Principles

Healing-centred principles

Bellis, M.A., Hughes, K., Leckenby, N. et al., 'Adverse childhood experiences and associations with health-harming behaviours in young adults: Surveys in eight eastern European countries' in *Bulletin of the World Health Organization*, 92(9), 641–655 (2014). Available from: DOI:10.2471/BLT.13.129247.

Centers for Disease Control and Prevention (CDC), *Adverse Childhood Experiences (ACEs)* (2021). [Online]. Available from: www.cdc.gov/violenceprevention/aces/ [accessed 24 November 2024].

Ginwright, S. 'The future of healing: Shifting from trauma-informed care to healing-centered engagement' in *Medium* (2018). [Online]. Available from: https://medium.com/@ginwright/the-future-of-healing-shifting-from-trauma-informed-care-to-healing-centered-engagement-634f557f4e4c [accessed 24 November 2024].

Treisman, K. *A Treasure Box for Creating Trauma-Informed Organizations: A Ready-to-Use Resource for Trauma, Adversity, and Culturally Informed, Infused and Responsive Systems* (2021). London: Jessica Kingsley Publishers.

Rhythm and ritual

Csikszentmihalyi, M. *Flow: The Psychology of Optimal Experience* (1990). New York: Harper & Row.

Van der Kolk, B.A. *The Body Keeps the Score: Brain, Mind, and Body in the Healing of Trauma* (2014). London: Penguin Books.

Collide and align
Brown, A.M. *Emergent Strategy: Shaping Change, Changing Worlds* (2017). Chico, CA: AK Press.

Cornell, J. *Joseph Cornell: Worlds in a Box* (2023). Revised Edition. London: Thames & Hudson.

Transition
Bridges, W. *Transitions: Making Sense of Life's Changes* (2004). Cambridge, MA: Da Capo Press.

Siegel, D. *The Mindful Therapist: A Clinician's Guide to Mindsight and Neural Integration* (2010). New York: W.W. Norton & Company.

Contribute and benefit
McKnight, J. and Block, P. *The Abundant Community: Awakening the Power of Families and Neighborhoods* (2010). San Francisco: Berrett-Koehler Publishers.

Simmons, D., Brackett, M.A. and Goleman, D. 'Emotional Intelligence and Community Resilience' in *Psychology Today* (2020). [Online]. Available from: www.psychologytoday.com/intl [accessed 24 November 2024].

Chapter 3: Doorway three: Process

Design thinking
British Design Council (n.d.) *The Double Diamond: A Universally Accepted Depiction of the Design Process*. Available from: www.designcouncil.org.uk/ [accessed 25 November 2024].

Collective action
Chang, C. (n.d.) Before I die project. Available from: https://beforeidieproject.com/ [accessed 25 November 2024].

Case study: Maff Potts

Potts, M. (n.d.) Camerados: Public Living Rooms. Available from: www.camerados.org/ [accessed 25 November 2024].

Systems thinking

Rockefeller Foundation, The Food Systems Map (2019). Available from: www.rockefellerfoundation.org/ [accessed 25 November 2024].

United Nations, Sustainable Development Goals (2015). Available from: www.un.org/sustainabledevelopment/ [accessed 25 November 2024].

Chapter 4: Doorway four: Practice

Healing

Ginwright, S. 'The future of healing: Shifting from trauma-informed care to healing-centered engagement' in *Medium* (2018). [Online]. Available from: https://medium.com/@ginwright/the-future-of-healing-shifting-from-trauma-informed-care-to-healing-centered-engagement-634f557f4e4c [accessed 24 November 2024].

Levine, P.A. *In an Unspoken Voice: How the Body Releases Trauma and Restores Goodness* (2010). Berkeley, CA: North Atlantic Books.

Tedeschi, R.G. and Calhoun, L.G. 'Posttraumatic growth: Conceptual foundations and empirical evidence' in *Psychological Inquiry*, 15(1), 1–18 (2004).

Thinking

Schön, D.A. *The Reflective Practitioner: How Professionals Think in Action* (1983). New York: Basic Books.

'Small and Mighty!' podcast series from the United Nations Trust Fund to End Violence against Women.

Watts, A. *The Book: On the Taboo Against Knowing Who You Are* (1972). New York: Vintage Books.

Leadership

Andrews, M. and McNamara, P. *Women and Social Action in Britain and Ireland: From the 1880s to the 1920s* (2005). London: Routledge.

Spade, D. *Mutual Aid: Building Solidarity During This Crisis (and the Next)* (2020). London: Verso Books.

'The Quartet' Philosophers (Anscombe, Foot, Midgley, Murdoch): Midgley, M. *The Ethical Primate: Humans, Freedom and Morality* (2002). London: Routledge.

Tending

McKnight, J. and Block, P. *The Abundant Community: Awakening the Power of Families and Neighborhoods* (2010). San Francisco, CA: Berrett-Koehler Publishers.

Rapp, C.A. and Goscha, R.J. *The Strengths Model: A Recovery-Oriented Approach to Mental Health Services.* 2nd ed. (2006). New York: Oxford University Press.

Nourishing

Spielberg, S. *Hook.* [Film] Directed by Steven Spielberg. (1991). USA: TriStar Pictures.

Chapter 5: Doorway five: Power

Poetry

Brown, A.M. *Emergent Strategy: Shaping Change, Changing Worlds* (2017). Chico, CA: AK Press.

Lorde, A. *Sister Outsider: Essays and Speeches* (1984). Freedom, CA: Crossing Press.

Desire paths

Bandura, A. *Social Learning Theory* (1977). Englewood Cliffs, NJ: Prentice Hall.

Odell, J. *How to Do Nothing: Resisting the Attention Economy* (2019). Brooklyn, NY: Melville House.

Power structures

Maslow, A.H. 'A Theory of Human Motivation' in *Psychological Review,* 50(4), 370–396 (1943).

VeneKlasen, L. and Miller, V. *A New Weave of Power, People & Politics: The Action Guide for Advocacy and Citizen Participation* (2002). Oklahoma City, OK: World Neighbors.

Ecosystem

Simard, S. *Finding the Mother Tree: Discovering the Wisdom of the Forest* (2021). London: Penguin Random House.

Magnetic support

Peterson, W.A. *The Art of Living* (1961). New York: Simon and Schuster.

Transformation Treasure Box

Brown, B. *The Gifts of Imperfection: Let Go of Who You Think You're Supposed to Be and Embrace Who You Are* (2010). Center City, MN: Hazelden Publishing.

The Plunge

Mindell, A. *Sitting in the Fire: Large Group Transformation Using Conflict and Diversity* (1995). Portland, OR: Lao Tse Press.

Index

A
A Brilliant Thing CIC xv–xvi, 42, 71, 119–120, 161, 193
abundant power 167
accountability 13–14
action learning sets 105
action-taking 129–133, 159
adverse childhood experiences (ACEs) 41
AI (Artificial Intelligence) 86
art making 52, 159, 193

B
backgrounds, understanding 76–77
balance 177
Bandura, Albert 180
'Before I Die' 102
being 136–139
'being in change' 137–138
belonging 100, 127–129
benefit, contribute and 43, 59–61, 129
big-picture thinking 88–93
blackberry jam 135
Boast Book xxii–xxiii
book clubs 107
boundaries 45, 49, 77, 131, 171
Brave Day 187–190
breaks, taking 161–163
 see also resting
brief, creating a 80–84
Brilliant Box 193, 194
British Design Council model 95–96
Brown, Adrienne Maree 60–61
Brown, Brene 177
burnout 131, 146, 161, 164

C
calm 137
Camerados 107, 109–114
Chang, Candy 102
charity model of aid 20
choice 5, 13, 43, 48–51, 65, 169
circles of tolerance 50–51
citizen assemblies 106
citizens 128
classism 9, 10
clay on the wheel 101
coaching 184
co-creation 42, 51, 112, 135
collaboration 15, 50, 91, 94, 99, 129, 178
collective action 99–108
collective power 5, 41, 166, 169, 173, 192
collide and align 43, 51–53
comfort and joy 147
command and control mechanisms 30
communities of practice 90
community organizing 104–108, 124, 140, 141–142
community soups 106
compassion 169–172
component parts 82, 84
conditioning 8–12, 19, 22, 29, 75, 161, 167, 170, 180
connections 32, 89, 97, 100, 165, 169–170, 172

conscious uncoupling 170
consensus 50
contribute and benefit 43, 59–61, 129
control, sense of 48, 99, 167
coping mechanisms 126, 127
co-production 16–17, 94, 99
co-regulation 153–154
Cornell, Joseph 52
creativity 2–3, 58–59, 76, 91, 119–120, 143, 158
Creedon, Beth 126
critical friends networks 105

D
daydreaming 17–19, 52, 84
decision-making processes 13, 16, 30, 50–51, 71
decluttering 148
depth 40, 183, 184
design challenge question 98–99
design thinking 42, 93–99, 160
designing reflection 66–67
desire paths 160–165
diagnose–medicate–operate path 29
diamond hand gesture 78
dimensional transformation 136
disconnecting 170
Discover, Define, Develop, Deliver design thinking 95–98
dissent and repair 51–52
diversity 53
Dodd, Ray 184
doing 129–133, 159
doorways and thresholds representing transitions x–xi
Dream Collage 66–67, 81, 82–83

E
ecosystem 175–179
education systems 84–86, 88
emails 162
emotion 121–126, 130, 137
empathy 17, 19, 26, 123, 170–171
endometriosis 5
energy 12, 21, 38, 56–57, 77, 82, 186
enrichment 149–150
equity 60
escaping from pain 3
exchange events 107

F
faith 148
fallow periods 44–45, 56
feelings 121–126, 130
filtering 43, 48–51, 65
Food Systems Map 89
forests 175–179
frames to dance within 72–77, 78, 83
freedom 12–17, 45

G
Galliano, Joseph 124
garden map 154–155
generational trauma 5, 41, 152
Ginwright, Dr Shawn 6–7
Gleaves, Caroline 195
'go-tos' 148
Grenfell Tower 29–31

H
hand gesture 78
healing power 166–169
healing-centered engagement 6–7
Healing-Centred Design framework xviii

outline xiv–xv
practice 117–155
principles 39–67
process 69–115
why use 32–33
healing-centred principles 40–48
helper/helped roles 20
Henderson, Kirstie 187–190
hidden qualities 185
hierarchy of needs 177
Hook 135–136
hurting bodies 28–29

I
ice cream machine 82
identity 127–129, 175, 176
imagination 12, 17, 19, 42, 58, 66, 84, 138
immersion 182–185
impulsiveness 64–65
inclusive communications teams 105
inequality 9, 10, 22
injustice 6, 9, 10
innovation 52, 160
intentionality 49, 57, 60, 65, 132, 138, 139, 169–172
intuition 53, 122, 143
Invitation xxiv–xxv, 193–195
isolation of pain 6

J
joy 26, 49, 89–93, 147

K
kindness, contagious 132

L
layering 145–150
leadership 124–126
Life Forest 175–179
'life score' activity 27

lighthouse learning 84–88
limitations 3, 4, 12, 81
Live Three Sixty 151–154
Lorde, Audre 159

M
Madgin, Alison 124–125
magnetic support 179–182
mass education 84–86
Matisse, Henri 81
mattering, sense of 26–27
me plus pain xxi
meaningful connections 49, 58
meaningful life 2–3, 4
medication 23, 29–31
memorable, making your work 102–103
mending, definition xii
Menstrual Health Project 33–37
momentum 21, 48, 64, 67, 70, 82, 98–99, 164
moving houses 11–12
murmurations 60–61, 105–106
mutual benefit/reciprocity 21, 43, 60, 125

N
navigating 138–139
needs, noticing your 164–165
needs hierarchy 177
neurodiversity 145–146, 160
neuroplasticity 31–32
nourishing 133–136

O
Obama, Barack 104
obsessions 183
Odell, Jenny 161
oppression 4, 5, 7, 13–14, 22, 122
organizing 14–15, 103–104
see also community organizing

organizing structures 105–108
overstimulation 145

P
pacing 56, 146
pain
  anatomy of 5–8
  doorway one 1–38
  escaping from pain 3
  isolation of pain 6
  me plus pain xxi
  pain management 21–26
  societal pain xxi, 7, 25–26, 29–30, 32, 40
  three states of xx–xxi
  understanding pain 7–8
pain to power transition xiv–xvi, 6–7, 36–37, 78, 108
painkillers 23, 29–31
participants 128–129
participatory action 128–129
participatory organizing 14–15
pausing 56–57
Person, Gabz 33–37
Peterson, Wilfred 181
plastic change 31–32
Plunge 182–185
poetry 158–160
political agendas 104
post-traumatic growth 41–42, 133–134
Potts, Maff 109–114
power
  abundant power 167
  activation of 158–195
  collective power 5, 41, 166, 169, 173, 192
  healing power 166–169
  multiple power sources 172–175
  'power with' 153
  structures 166–169

Power Landscape 174
practice 117–155
principles 39–67
priority setting 45
  see also filtering
privilege 173
protection 177
Public Living Rooms 107, 109–114
purpose, finding 42, 59

Q
Quartet, The 124
Quest Notes 38
quick fixes 133

R
racism 9, 10, 11, 13–14, 41
Random Acts of Kindness 132
Rapp, Charles 140
raw ingredients 81, 83, 101
Reciprocal Determinism 180
reflective practice 17–19, 37–38, 66–67, 114–115, 119–120, 154–155, 191–192
reflective practice forums 105
relationships
  feelings 123
  healing 44
  isolation 164
  meaningful connections 49, 58
  mutual benefit/reciprocity 21, 43, 60, 125
  spaces of belonging 100, 127–129
  see also connections
releasing 37–38, 122
resilience factors 41, 135
responsibilities 13–14
resting 3, 53, 57, 129–130
restorative justice 15–16
Restructure Ritual 186, 191–192

revolution, floods of 19–21
revolution leaders 124–125
rhythm and ritual 43, 44–48, 51, 55, 56, 159–160
rights 13–14
Roll to Recovery 62–66
rules, sticking to the 8–9

S
scaffolding 11, 12, 70
Self-Compassion Basketball xxii
self-development 44
Seligman, Martin 140
sense of control 48, 99, 167
sexism 10, 14, 35
shadow sides 159
showing up 101, 125
silk filters 49–50
Simard, Suzanne 176
Simon, Herbert 95
Smith, Keri 75
social connections 26
  see also relationships
social enterprises 104
Social Learning Theory 180
societal pain xxi, 7, 25–26, 29–30, 32, 40
soft strengths 139–145
solidarity 100
spaces of belonging 100
spaciousness 148
statistics on chronic pain 4
strengths based approaches 140–141, 173
stress messages 164
'strong suit' 126
support, magnetic 179–182
supporting needs 28
symbolic actions 47, 54
symbol-seeking 114–115
systems mapping 88–93
systems thinking 88–92, 99

T
talismans 55–56
tending xii–xiii, 139–150
thematic networks 106
thinking xxii, 126–127, 181
Thomas, Tamu 151–154
thoughts, paying attention to xxii
tolerance 169–172
Transformation Treasure Box 185–186
transforming
  definition xiii–xiv
  transformation-focused change xi
  vision for transformation 81–82, 83
  where and when 150
  why xiv–xv
transition 43, 53–59
trauma
  post-traumatic growth 41–42, 133–134
  societal pain 40–41
  trauma-informed work xvi, 6, 42, 43–44, 77
  trauma-responsive places 42
treasures x
Treisman, Dr Karen 42–43
trust 44, 63, 64–65, 66, 73, 99, 123, 131

U
undercover leaders 125–126
understanding pain 7–8
'Unfold your story' 27–28

V
visibility of actions 131–133
vision for transformation 81–82, 83
vulnerability 177

W
Wayfinding Inc. 174
Weetman, Michael 62–66
western medicine 28

whole life healing 26–32
wide stance, soft focus 101–102
Windgassen, Dr Sula xviii–xxiii
Wrasama, Kathleen 124

A quick word from Practical Inspiration Publishing...

We hope you found this book both practical and inspiring – that's what we aim for with every book we publish.

We publish titles on topics ranging from leadership, entrepreneurship, HR and marketing to self-development and wellbeing.

Find details of all our books at: www.practicalinspiration.com

Did you know...

We can offer discounts on bulk sales of all our titles – ideal if you want to use them for training purposes, corporate giveaways or simply because you feel these ideas deserve to be shared with your network.

We can even produce bespoke versions of our books, for example with your organization's logo and/or a tailored foreword.

To discuss further, contact us on info@practicalinspiration.com.

Got an idea for a business book?

We may be able to help. Find out more about publishing in partnership with us at: bit.ly/PIpublishing.

Follow us on social media...

- @PIPTalking
- @pip_talking
- @practicalinspiration
- @piptalking
- Practical Inspiration Publishing